ADDISON-WESLEY EARLY CHILDHOOD EDUCATION

CHILDREN'S PLAY

An Introduction for Care Providers

ADDISON-WESLEY EARLY CHILDHOOD EDUCATION

CHILDREN'S PLAY

An Introduction for Care Providers

Vicki Mulligan

Addison-Wesley Publishers Limited

Don Mills, Ontario • Reading, Massachusetts
Menlo Park, California • New York • Wokingham, England
Amsterdam • Bonn • Sydney • Singapore • Tokyo
Madrid • San Juan • Paris • Seoul • Milan • Mexico City • Taipei

Dedication

For my childhood playmates
Patricia, Maureen, and Valerie

Executive Editor: Joseph Gladstone
Managing Editor: Linda Scott
Editor: Anne Norman, West Coast Editorial Associates
Coordinating Editor: Madhu Ranadive
Design and Page Layout: Maria Modopoulos
Production Coordinator: Melanie van Rensburg
Manufacturing Coordinator: Sharon Latta Paterson
Cover Design: Anthony Leung

Photos on pages 1, 17, 31, 49, 67, 89, 131, 149, and 159 courtesy of Beth Norton. Cover photo by Deborah Maunder. Photo on page 109 provided by the author.

Canadian Cataloguing in Publication Data

Mulligan, Vicki Bridge, 1948–
          Children's play — an introduction for care providers

Includes bibliographical references and index.
ISBN 0-201-82979-7

1. Play.   2. Child care.   I. Title.

HQ782.M85 1996   649'.5   C95-933204-9

ISBN 0-201-82979-7

Printed and bound in Canada by Webcom.

A B C D E -WC- 00 99 98 97 96

◆ ◆ ◆ Table of Contents

Preface

Supporting children's play involves the creative blending of the care provider's knowledge and skills. Caring for children is an expression of the care provider's individuality as well as an application of professional expertise. High-quality play programs are tailored to the individual children they serve. The care provider is not replicating any other program, using a pattern, or following a script to produce high-quality child care. This book is based on the assumption that supporting children's play involves the continuous application of the care provider's professional judgment. There are no proven recipes for excellent play programs that suit all children. This book introduces care providers to some of the factors to be weighed when making decisions affecting children's play, and it proposes that care providers conduct their own research in order to expand the profession's understanding of children's play.

Chapter 1 introduces the themes that are woven through the book. It also discusses the poor fit between most of the research literature on the subject of play and the needs of care providers. Chapter 2 summarizes existing theories of play and points out their limitations. Care providers are encouraged to use their own perspectives on children's play to develop the next generation of theories of play. In Chapter 3, inclusive play environments are described and their benefits are identified. Chapter 3 also discusses the characteristics required of care providers who work in inclusive play environments. Chapter 4 adds a new element to the discussion of quality play environments—local appropriateness. Local appropriateness is defined and steps for creating a locally appropriate program are outlined. Chapters 5, 6, and 7 discuss ways of supporting the play of infants and toddlers, preschoolers, and school-age children respectively. The development of typical children in each age group is summarized and age-appropriate play environments are described. Chapter 8 discusses the issues of adult intervention in children's play, the facilitation of peer friendships, and the teaching of social skills. Information is presented to assist care providers in making personal decisions on each of these issues. Chapter 9 focuses on hurtful play, sex play, and play that suggests possible abuse. Each type of play is discussed and care provider responses are suggested. The book's final chapter is devoted to the selection of playthings. This topic is addressed last because it requires care providers to synthesize, integrate, and apply all of their knowledge of play. The factors to be considered when selecting playthings are identified and discussed.

Although this book's focus is children's play, readers are encouraged to look at play and other elements of professional child care practice through a wide-angle lens. Play environments exist within communities and they reveal community values and priorities. The decisions and actions of care providers in those play environments have an impact that extends beyond the children and the child care facility. Care providers are encouraged to see themselves operating within this larger context, contributing to the overall quality of community life.

This book is intended for use as a teaching and learning resource. It includes design features that assist learners. For example, objectives are stated at the beginning of each chapter and there is a summary section entitled *Chapter in a Nutshell* at the end of each chapter. The *At Practicum*, *Extend Your Learning*, and *Look Inward* sections of each chapter contain learning activities and questions that stimulate introspection and self-awareness. An Instructor's Guide containing teaching methodologies, additional learning activities, and evaluation techniques is available to instructors from the publisher.

Acknowledgments

While writing this book I was supported, encouraged, counseled, assisted, guided, and cared for by many people.

I am grateful to Linda Leone for sharing with me perspectives drawn from her experiences caring for children and teaching future care providers. Linda's enthusiastic responses to each draft provided me with encouragement throughout the writing process. I thank Linda for acting as my early childhood education consultant.

I also received thoughtful, constructive reactions to early drafts from Jan Blazall, Wendy Fletcher, Kathy Harrison, Dawn Hedley, Deborah Maunder, Linda McDonell, Barbara Stewart, and Vera Wise. Their suggestions, comments, and questions were very helpful to me and I thank them for their insightful analyses and guidance.

I sincerely appreciate Maureen Lightfoot's contributions. Maureen skillfully and patiently did all of the word processing involved in the book's evolution from pencil-written manuscript to its final form. I am also grateful for the help of Violet Bridge who proofread the early drafts.

This book gave me the opportunity once again to work with editor Anne Norman. Anne's assistance was invaluable and working with her was a pleasure.

I am grateful Lene Gregersen and Lauréanne Lepage of the Victoria Children's Centre, Katherine Beecroft of Lakehill Preschool, Darcelle Cottons, Administrator of UBC Child Care Services, and all of the UBC Child Care staff for their cooperation during my quest for photographs of children at play. I appreciate the skill and artistry of Deborah Maunder and Beth Norton who captured in their photographs the play of Anita Proom and all of the other children. I thank the parents who generously gave me permission to use photographs of their children.

It was possible for me to write this book because of the support I receive from my family. My husband Robert and our son Michael maintain the caring ambiance that sustains me. Michael's assistance with the library research and his computer expertise are also greatly appreciated.

Vicki Mulligan

1 Introduction to Play

Objectives

◆ to introduce the themes that are woven throughout this book

◆ to identify some of the drawbacks of relying exclusively on the human development literature for guidance in planning play programs for children

◆ to introduce play in the context of child care programs

❖ ❖ ❖ ❖ Care Providers

This book has been written primarily for care providers—the individuals who care for and educate infants, toddlers, preschoolers, and school-age children in the children's homes, child care centers, family day care homes, preschools, community centers, and before- and after-school care programs. Care providers are known by various titles according to local preferences and traditions. You may be training to become an early childhood educator, a preschool teacher, a child care worker, an educarer, a school-age care provider, a family day care operator, a nanny, or a recreation leader, or you may already work in one of those jobs. Or you may be reading this book as a parent interested in enhancing your own children's play. Whatever your situation, I hope that you will find practical information here that will help you do a better, more satisfying job.

❖ ❖ ❖ ❖ Themes

Throughout this book several themes will appear again and again. You will encounter repeated references to

◆ the *relationship* between the care provider and the child

◆ *ethical* child care practice

◆ *locally appropriate* child care practice

◆ the *research practitioner* role of the care provider

Adult-Child Relationships

Adults who work with children have the opportunity to form close and caring relationships with those children. The quality of the adult-child relationships distinguishes excellent care and education programs from the mediocre. Care providers who support and enhance children's play do so within warm, nurturing relationships. Your relationships with the children in your care profoundly influence their development. Through their relationships with you, children can develop essential social skills and satisfy their emotional needs. The relationship between care provider and child is not a one-way relationship involving only adult giving, teaching, and supporting. Caring relationships with children can also be a source of deep satisfaction and joy for you.

As you read, you will be learning some of the factors to consider when you plan for and support children's play. You will learn about appropriate play materials and environments. The provision of play materials and suitable environments are, of course, important aspects of the care provider's job. They are, however, secondary to the formation of warm relationships with the children—relationships that allow them to explore, to learn, to trust, and to experience the acceptance and caring of another human being. This book will focus repeatedly on those relationships.

Ethical Decision Making

Adults who work with children are continually called on to make decisions that are partly or exclusively in the ethical domain. These are decisions that involve choosing the right action when the welfare of people is at stake. We make decisions in the ethical domain based on our ideas about how people ought to behave, how we ought to treat one another, and what our obligations are to people. Planning and guiding children's play involves the application of the care provider's knowledge and skills. It also involves the application of the care provider's personal and professional ethical principles.

As you read, you will be learning what theorists have proposed and what researchers have discovered about children's play. However, the scholarly literature on play offers no guidance on the ethical issues intertwined with child care practice. This book addresses the ethical problems and dilemmas that are part of the job of working with children. It will help you to clarify the ethical principles that will serve as the foundation for your practice.

Locally Appropriate Practice

The discussions of planning for play begin with the assumption that high-quality child care programs do not come in a one-size-fits-all package. Excellent programs are "locally appropriate"—that is, they reflect the communities they serve. The cultural traditions, the values, and the way of life of the families are incorporated into locally appropriate child care programs. It is not possible to select from a textbook a play program that will fit the community in which you work. Care providers in locally appropriate programs begin with an awareness of their profession's shared body of knowledge and standards of practice, but they tailor their programs to suit local families and the community. Locally appropriate child care programs are developed in consultation with parents and other interested community members, and they support the needs and priorities of parents. They introduce children to local people and activities. They reflect the children's heritage and familiarize children with their communities.

This book will help you to plan a locally appropriate program. You will learn to look for and identify the best features of your community and build them into your child care program. Locally appropriate practice is discussed in detail in Chapter 4.

The Care Provider as a Research Practitioner

The research literature on the topic of play is largely unhelpful to care providers. Although it does contain some nuggets of value to the people who are responsible for the care and education of children, most of it is only of interest to other researchers. The scholars who have studied play have, for the most part, done so to answer research questions unrelated to child care practice. Very little of this research is of practical value to care providers. In many of these studies, play has been a dependent variable. In other words, children's play was not the focus of the research. In a comprehensive review of the research on play, Fromberg (1992) identified some of the limitations of this body of literature. The overall lack of relevance of the play research to care providers is partly related to the weaknesses that Fromberg pointed out: the small numbers of subjects in most of the experimental studies, the fact that most of the play studies have been carried out in laboratory settings for brief periods of time, the focus on solitary players, and the concentration on single dimensions such as the affective, cognitive, social, or linguistic aspects of play.

Care providers are in a position to make a major contribution to our collective understanding of children's play. Care providers can learn much from the play of the children in their own programs. They can observe children's play and answer questions about play that matter to practitioners and that have significance to individual programs. The information gathered by care providers can also be shared with colleagues and others. "Research practitioner" is a name for these front-line care providers who actively observe children in their own facilities, reflect on their day-to-day practice, and share their conclusions with other care providers.

This book advocates that care providers conduct research that is important to them and to their profession. As you read, you will be encouraged to think of research as part of the role of a professional care provider. Later, your own research could deepen your understanding of your program design and practice and by sharing your research, you will enable other care providers to learn from you (see Box 1.1). Over time, the profession will develop a rich literature of its own to document the experiences and learning of its members.

Box 1.1
Telling Our Stories

The knowledge, understandings, and insights care providers gain from their relationships with children have qualities not found in traditional research studies. Knowledge acquired on the inside of relationships is personal and intimate and revealing of ourselves. It has a texture quite unlike the findings of a scientific research study.

To share this inside knowledge, care providers may use formats that differ from the format used by research specialists. The discoveries of research practitioners lend themselves to narrative formats— stories as opposed to reports. Stories can accommodate the emotions and meanderings of relationships. They have the flexibility to allow us to describe paths to knowledge that are neither direct nor sequential. Care providers' stories represent a large untapped source of wisdom.

Working as a research practitioner involves approaching children's play with a distinctive attitude. The research practitioner approaches the situation as a learning opportunity. The research practitioner's observations of children are not motivated just by the need to supervise them to ensure their safety or to provide assistance and support. The research practitioner is also advancing his or her knowledge—observing the children's behavior in order to better understand them and observing their use of the play environment in order to evaluate its appropriateness. This "active observing" is actually research. The research practitioner is gathering knowledge, adding to his or her understanding of the children and their play. This knowledge is applied when the care provider interacts with children and makes improvements to the play environment. The active observing of research practitioners is a legitimate source of valuable, practical knowledge.

◆ ◆ ◆ ◆ Play and Human Development Theories

The child care profession has drawn many of its essential tenets from the work of developmental psychologists. Human development theories and research provide the rationale for many aspects of child care practice. The National Association for the Education of Young Children (NAEYC) has taken the lead in synthesizing the relevant human development literature and making it accessible to care providers. The NAEYC position is that "a major determinant of program quality is the extent to which knowledge of child development is applied in program practices—the degree to which the program is *developmentally appropriate*" (Bredekamp, 1987). The NAEYC guidelines for developmentally appropriate practice have been widely disseminated and are incorporated into many care and education programs for young children. Project Home Safe has developed comparable principles for child care programs for school-age children (Albrecht & Plantz, 1993). Together, the NAEYC and Project Home Safe advocate that care providers work with children in ways that are supported by or extrapolated from the human development literature.

Attitudes Toward Play

The present primacy of the concept of developmental appropriateness in child care practice is reflected in prevailing attitudes toward play. The place of play in care and education programs has been justified in terms of how play contributes to children's development. Play initiated and directed by children is represented as the perfect developmentally appropriate activity. The prevailing play framework, influenced by theories of human development, assumes that adults ought to help children move forward on the various developmental continua described in these theories. Play is viewed as worthwhile because it is seen as supporting the movement forward to more advanced levels and stages. In other words, play is viewed as a means of stimulating children's progress. Many advocates of play emphasize its usefulness in promoting children's development. This view—emphasizing the usefulness of play and its value as a means of moving children to higher developmental stages—is widespread (see Box 1.2).

Advocating play because it promotes a more serious objective such as development is consistent with the ambivalence with which many North Americans regard frivolous activity. Saracho (1991) sees the characterization of play as "child's work" as a means of justifying play in a society with a strong work ethic. The view that play is worthwhile because it enables children to advance or develop is intertwined with our cultural values. Focusing on play's utility in achieving a serious goal such as stimulating development, we have been overlooking its capacity to produce joy, pleasure, and happiness for children. The fact that play is seldom promoted primarily as a source of enjoyment reveals the priorities of North American adults.

Box 1.2

Developmental Appropriateness

Although developmental appropriateness is widely accepted as a principle of child care practice, it is not unconditionally endorsed by all members of the child care profession. Spodek (1991) acknowledges the primacy of the concept of developmentally appropriate practice when he calls it "the new orthodoxy" (p. 12). Spodek is critical of the tendency to make developmental appropriateness the only criterion for judging early childhood curricula. He expresses concern that our emphasis on developmental appropriateness results in insufficient attention being paid to curriculum content.

continued

Bloch's (1992) concerns about using developmental psychology as the primary foundation for child care practice are more fundamental. She questions the basic assumptions on which child development research is based. She criticizes the dominance of positivist, empirical-analytical research frameworks, which emulate the "hard" physical sciences. She argues that child care research ought to include alternative research approaches as well. Bloch does not write off human development theories and research. Her position is that child care providers rely on them unduly, to the detriment of both the profession and the children. Bloch states that one of the drawbacks of relying on developmental psychology is that there is not enough attention paid to the societal influences that oppress children and cause inequities in achievement. Bloch is encouraging us to think about children in relation to the larger society in which they live. She is advocating that care providers take a broad perspective on all of the influences on children's development.

Developmental Psychology and Child Care Practice

The strong influence of developmental psychology has been a mixed blessing for front-line care providers responsible for planning and implementing play programs for groups of children. Developmental theories and research have provided care providers with a body of scholarly work from which child care curriculum models and standards of practice have been drawn. For a young profession, lacking an integrated theory of play and seeking a respectable, research-supported basis for practice, developmental psychology seemed to fill the bill. However, the fit is not entirely satisfactory. The published developmental norms used to define age-appropriateness cannot be generalized to all children. Like all research findings, these norms reflect characteristics of particular groups of subjects. Care providers working with children who differ (culturally or otherwise) from the children who served as subjects in the research studies must consciously avoid interpreting differences as deficits. Once sensitized to this concern, conscientious care providers do interpret child development research findings cautiously.

Less easily resolved is the problem of the research questions that are addressed by developmental psychologists. The issues investigated and the methodologies used when they study children's play naturally reflect their own professional perspectives and priorities. Unfortunately, these rarely match the needs of care providers. Hundreds of the published studies of aspects of children's play are irrelevant to care providers, who face the challenge of planning and supporting play experiences for groups of children. This is not a criticism of the research. Many of the studies are wonderful examples of developmental psychology. They simply focus on different questions than the ones care providers need to have answered.

The extensive lists of references accompanying Fromberg's (1992) and Rubin, Fein, and Vandenberg's (1983) reviews of the play research are dominated by research studies that focus on issues that are important to psychologists seeking to understand children and their play. The studies represent basic research. For example, Fromberg describes an approach to social play known as the "script model." Many researchers have studied the structure and context of children's make-believe play using this model. The script theory research contains terms such as "cognitive templates," "affective representational templates," "cognitive seeds," and "mental models." This type of research is primarily of interest to and understood by other researchers. A front-line care provider wishing to give a group of preschoolers opportunities for make-believe play would be unlikely to read, let alone apply, this type of research. The intent here is not to dismiss the value of the research or to question the work of scholars who have studied the script model or any other aspect of children's play. This is simply an illustration of the differences between the priorities of researchers and care providers.

The gap between the human development scholarly literature on play and the needs of care providers is a wide one. It is particularly noticeable in the area of school-age child care. In preparing its principles of developmentally appropriate practice in school-age child care programs, Project Home Safe "*extrapolated* [emphasis added] from theoretical thinking, from developmental research on school-age children, and from practice" (Albrecht & Plantz, 1993, p. viii). In other words, the research did not directly address the care provider's questions concerning appropriate practice.

The research literature on play is always expanding. Someday human development scholars may conduct studies that will guide child care practitioners. For the time being, however, we should have modest expectations when we look to the existing research for guidance and insights on how to most appropriately support children's play. The lack of a strong practice-oriented research base is the reason why it is important for care providers to become researchers and develop a specialized body of literature that focuses on issues of concern to practitioners (see Box 1.3).

Box 1.3
An Alternative Approach

Kelly-Byrne (1989) has criticized the assumptions and research methodologies of the psychologists who have studied children's play. As an alternative to the approaches of most of the researchers, she advocates the use of an "interpretive science model" as a way of gaining understanding of play. Kelly-Byrne describes the proposed model in this way:

> *In contrast to a natural science model of behavior, the interpretive science model posits an interest in persons as agents (not objects), in intentional acts (not simply the behavior), and in understanding the human world (rather than predicting and controlling events). (p. 8)*

If scholars choose to follow Kelly-Byrne's advice and study play from a different perspective, they may indeed develop understandings that will be of value to child care practitioners. However, the interpretive studies of play called for by Kelly-Byrne have yet to be done. Rather than waiting for scholars to conduct such studies, care providers might begin to conduct their own studies as research practitioners.

◆ ◆ ◆ ◆ **Play in the Child Care Context**

Planning for and supporting children's play are among the most enjoyable aspects of working with children (see Box 1.4). This book is intended to deepen your understanding of play and prepare you to confidently approach this facet of your job. One of the characteristics of a satisfying professional practice is the practitioner's ability not only to do a job well but also to understand and explain the reasons for particular practices. The chapters that follow will help you to plan for and support children's play. They will also give you a framework for assessing the appropriateness of the play programs you observe during practicum visits and the recommendations you read in publications dealing with play. You will also be encouraged to reflect on your own practice to articulate a rationale for your practice on the basis of ethical principles and professional standards.

Play is at the heart of excellent child care programs. There are instruments designed to assess quality such as the *Infant/Toddler Environment Rating Scale* (Harms, Cryer, & Clifford, 1990), the *Family Day Care Rating Scale* (Harms & Clifford, 1989), and the *Early Childhood Environment Rating Scale* (Harms & Clifford, 1980). These all include evaluations of the extent to which children have the opportunities and materials needed for play. Published descriptions of quality such as the Canadian Child Care Federation's (1994) *National Statement on Quality Child Care*, Project Home Safe's *Quality Criteria for School-Age Child Care Programs* (Albrecht, 1991), and the NAEYC's position statement on developmentally appropriate practice (Bredekamp, 1987) acknowledge the importance of play as a major component of child care programs. Care providers who work with children of all ages and in all settings spend much of their time planning for and supporting play. This book will assist you in preparing to assume this responsibility.

Box 1.4
What Is Play?

"Play is the child's art form, the vehicle for creative expression, the primary avenue to learning and development, a source of joy and contentment."

– J. L. Frost (1985), p. ix

"Play is existential, to do with life."

– B. Sutton-Smith (1994)

"Play is a form of communication."

– D. Kelly-Byrne (1989), p. 11

"Young children's play is:
Symbolic, in that it represents reality with an 'as if' or 'what if' attitude

Meaningful, in that it connects or relates experiences

Active, in that children are doing things

continued

> *Pleasurable*, even when children are engaged seriously in activity
>
> *Voluntary* and *intrinsically motivated*, whether the motives are curiosity, mastery, affiliation, or others
>
> *Rule-governed*, whether implicitly or explicitly expressed
>
> *Episodic*, characterized by emerging and shifting goals that children develop spontaneously."
>
> — D. P. Fromberg (1992), p. 43

Although the instruments designed to assess child care quality and the descriptions of quality programs all encourage adults to give children time, space, materials, and encouragement to play, there is less consensus in the play literature on the question of why we should support and encourage children's play. The various answers to the question "Why encourage or support play?" reflect respondents' assumptions, values, and goals for children. As you read this book, you are asked to reflect on and clarify your own assumptions, values, and goals for children's play. The "Look Inward" sections at the end of each chapter will assist you in becoming more self-aware. One of the goals of the book is that you will gain insights into both how to plan for and support children's play and why you chose particular ways of doing so.

◆ ◆ ◆ ◆ Chapter 1 in a Nutshell

The following major understandings were introduced in Chapter 1:

◆ Warm, caring adult-child relationships are an essential element of high-quality child care.

◆ Care providers constantly make ethical choices.

◆ Excellent child care programs are locally appropriate.

◆ Care providers can contribute to the understanding of children's play by becoming research practitioners.

◆ Children's play is usually defended in terms of its contribution to their development.

- Care providers have primarily looked to developmental psychology for theories and research to guide their practice.

- The existing body of scholarly literature on the subject of children's play is of limited value to care providers.

At Practicum

1. Watch a care provider interact with a child who is playing. Notice the care provider's words, tone of voice, facial expression, distance from the child, and body language. Notice how the child responds to the care provider. Based on your observations, list some words that describe the quality of their relationship.

2. Speak with your sponsor care provider. Ask your sponsor how he or she justifies play to parents. What explanations does he or she give when parents question the amount of time devoted to play? Following your conversation, make brief notes summarizing your sponsor's rationale for play. Classify the arguments your sponsor uses to justify play. Put check marks beside the arguments that focus on play's contribution to children's development. Put stars beside other reasons for allowing children time to play.

3. Look for an example of an adult doing or saying something that is supportive of a child's play. Choose an interaction that you feel is an example of appropriate practice. Briefly describe the adult's behavior in your notebook. After reading this book, return to your description to see if you still consider this adult's behavior to be an appropriate way of supporting the child's play.

◆ ◆ ◆ ◆ Extend Your Learning

1. The *Infant/Toddler Environment Rating Scale* (Harms, Cryer, & Clifford, 1990) identifies criteria for evaluating how well a child care program supports the active physical play of infants and toddlers. A program would have a "Good" rating for active physical play if it had these features:

    ◆ Convenient outdoor area where infants/toddlers are separated from older children used for at least one hour daily year-round, except in very bad weather.

    ◆ All toys and equipment for physical activity used both indoors and outdoors are age-appropriate.

    ◆ Materials used daily stimulate a variety of large muscle skills (Ex. crawling, walking, balancing, climbing, ball play).

    ◆ Active play areas are not crowded. (p. 25)

    A program would receive an "Excellent" rating if it had all of the "Good" features plus these "Excellent" features:

    ◆ Physical play equipment changed or rotated weekly to provide new challenges either indoors or outdoors (Ex. crawling tunnel, games with bean bags, tumbling on mat, ball games).

    ◆ Caregiver talks to children about their activities (Ex. explains safety rules, names up/down, in/out). (p. 25)

    To the preceding description of an "Excellent" program, add some criteria that indicate high-quality *relationships* between the adult and the children.

2. The literature on children's play includes many different definitions of play. Collect the definitions used by any three authors who have written about children's play. Record the definitions along with the names of the authors and full citations for the publications in which they appeared. Which of these definitions is most useful to care providers?

3. If you have access to a college library, find and read a journal article that includes the word "play" in the title. Summarize the results of that study in one page or less.

If you do not have access to a college library, find and read an article on play in a parenting magazine. You can find parenting magazines in public libraries and on newsstands. Summarize that article in one page or less.

Would the article you summarized help you plan appropriate play experiences for a group of four-year-olds?

◆ ◆ ◆ ◆ # Look Inward

If you are using this book as a textbook for a course, you will not be asked to share your answers to these questions with your instructor or classmates. These questions are provided to stimulate introspection.

1. Clarify your beliefs regarding play by finishing these sentences in your notebook:

    a. When children play, they . . .

    b. When children are playing, adults should . . .

    c. Children need time to play because . . .

    As you read this book return to your sentence endings periodically to see if any of your beliefs have changed.

2. Recall your own childhood experiences.

    a. What is your earliest memory of play?

    b. Can you recall playing alone when you were a preschooler?

    c. Can you recall playing with another child or group of children?

    What emotions did you feel in each of these play experiences?

3. Recall a relationship between yourself as a young child and an adult who was responsible for your care. Think of three or four words that describe that relationship. In your adult role as a care provider, are there positive features of that relationship that you should try to replicate? Are there negative features of that relationship that you should try to avoid repeating?

Theoretical Perspectives on Play

Objectives

◆ to introduce some of the historical and contemporary theories of play

◆ to identify some of the influences of play theories on child care practices

◆ to discuss some of the limitations and criticisms of prevailing theories of play

◆ to propose that care providers begin to generate new theories of play

 # Theory Building

All branches of the social and natural sciences include theories. Each theory provides an overarching explanation of what is known about its subject. Good theories tie together the findings of all of the research in a given field. The theories are supported by data gained from research, and they in turn stimulate research as scholars devise experiments that test predictions based on the theories. Theories are particularly important in the world of scholarly research. A theory provides researchers with a framework to which they can add the data they collect. Over time a theory may be so well supported by data that people in the field consider it to be valid and no longer test it empirically. Alternatively, over time a theory may fall out of favor as researchers gather data that are at odds with the predictions based on the theory. Although these out-of-favor theories are known to be incorrect, they provide an interesting historical context for the fields in which they developed.

In many branches of science the process of generating theories, testing them empirically, and accepting or replacing them is well established. You may remember studying theories in science courses you have taken. You probably learned how human understanding of the universe has grown as scientists conducted experiments that either supported or disproved the theories of the day. A theory provides people with a starting point or point of view from which to examine a topic. It explains what is already known and it enables us to develop hypotheses for future experiments.

The process of generating and testing theories has taken place in the study of play. In contrast with the theory building and research in many other areas of academic study, the study of play is still at a relatively early stage. It does not yet have a strong, comprehensive theory that synthesizes all that is known about play. The published theories of play have limitations. Each provides an incomplete framework for both academics studying play and care providers planning play programs for children.

◆ ◆ ◆ ◆ Early Theories of Play

Wortham (1985) has outlined the leading theories of play of the twentieth century. She identified four theories that were influential between 1900 and 1930: the surplus energy theory, the recreation theory, the instinct theory, and the recapitulation theory. These early theories attempted to explain why children play.

◆ According to the surplus energy theory, children play in order to get rid of or run off leftover energy.

◆ Energy is also the focus of the recreation theory. However, it describes play as a way of restoring energy and helping people recover from fatigue caused by work.

◆ According to the instinct theory, children's play is considered to be a natural, inherited behavior. The instinct theorists saw the play of children and young animals as preparing them for adult life.

◆ The recapitulation theory of play also assumes that play is an inherited behavior and a rehearsal for adult life. However, the recapitulation theory reflects a Darwinian influence, with children's stages of play viewed as repeating the stages of human evolution.

Frost (1992) has criticized all of these early theories. He points out that they are not founded on systematic observation or scientific data. Ellis (1973) has described them as "armchair theories" (p. 24). Certainly they do not provide us with an overarching explanation of children's play, and all of these early theories are now regarded by play scholars as inadequate. Although they are no longer accepted, Frost feels these early theories of play have left behind a lamentable legacy. He blames these discredited theories for the poor-quality play environments presently available to North American children. Frost regrets the lingering influence of these theories: "Many practitioners at the present time still consider play a waste of time or an avenue to let off steam, and they construct play environments that are poorly suited to children's cognitive, social, affective, and psychomotor needs" (p. 10). In Frost's opinion, the cumulative effect of these early theories was to communicate that "play, like childhood, is unimportant" (p. 13).

Frost's interpretation probably overstates the negative influence of these early theories. Rather than denying the importance of play, they can be seen as first steps in an area that had not previously been studied. The early theories of play may be regarded as establishing play as an important topic that deserves our serious thought and attention.

◆ ◆ ◆ ◆ The Second Generation of Theories of Play

The three major theories of play that have dominated the years since 1930 are all offshoots of theories of psychology. These second-generation theories are more sophisticated and complex than the early theories. Unlike the early theories, the second-generation theories have stimulated a large number of research studies and they continue to exert a significant influence on child care practices.

The psychoanalytic theory, the cognitive-developmental theory, and the behavioral theory in psychology all have derivative theories of play. You may have been introduced to these psychology theories in your child development courses. Each theory presents a different perspective on human behavior. A detailed description of these psychology theories is beyond the scope of this book. You can learn more about them in most introductory psychology textbooks and most child development textbooks. Our focus here is on the theories of play that have their roots in those perspectives.

The Psychoanalytic Theory of Play

The psychoanalytic theory describes personality development. This theory originated with the work of Freud. Some of the terms central to the psychoanalytic theory have now become part of mainstream English, with concepts such as id, ego, and superego used and understood far beyond the field of psychology. Freud and others who articulated the psychoanalytic perspective looked at children's play and its role in ego development. They believed that play reduced children's anxieties, and was therefore considered to be therapeutic. In make-believe play, children work through and gain control of their emotions. In other words, by expressing and releasing emotions in play, the child becomes psychologically stronger and healthier. From this theoretical perspective evolved the play therapy approach to working with troubled children (see Box 2.1).

Box 2.1
Play Therapy

Although the roots of play therapy can be traced back to psychoanalysts of the 1920s and 1930s, play therapists today approach their work from many different theoretical perspectives. Play therapists today are a very diverse group and they use a variety of strategies. Miller (1984) defines play therapy as

participation by the child in a play setting, with an attendant adult, wherein the child is given the optimal opportunity to utilize what is a natural and enjoyable medium (play) for the purpose of helping the child to resolve the problems of modern living. (p. 85)

Play therapy is intended to help children express and cope with their feelings. Many play therapists approach their work with the belief that play is inherently healing. They provide play environments, establish relationships with their clients, and observe, interpret, and discuss the play that occurs.

It is difficult to evaluate how and why play therapy is effective. Reported beneficial outcomes may be due to the play therapist's particular theoretical approach and methods, to the play experience, or to the caring relationship.

The psychoanalytic theory of play has practical implications for care providers. From the perspective of this theory, children's play is seen as having a significant impact on their personality development. Care providers who accept this theoretical perspective provide children with opportunities to play in order to ensure their emotional well-being. Since the play itself is valued, the care provider's primary role is to let the play happen. From this perspective, the emotional benefits are seen as being derived from the play rather than from the adult-child relationship. Care providers who base their practice on this theory tend to stand back from children's play in order to avoid impeding the ego development that is taking place.

The psychoanalytic perspective on play looks at play as an opportunity for children to express their emotions. This approach continues to influence the practice of many care providers. Although today's training for care providers does not encourage them to adopt a psychoanalytic approach, there remains in the profession a reluctance to become involved in children's play. Feeney (1992) points out that before the 1960s adults were taught to keep out of children's play. It was believed that children were resolving inner conflicts through their play and adult interference would be detrimental to the children's psychological development. Feeney explains that during that period "the only valid role allocated to the teacher was that of creator of the environment and careful observer of children's actions within the prepared environment" (p. 160). Although care providers today may not state their positions in psychoanalytic terms, many feel it is inappropriate and possibly harmful for adults to intrude when children are playing. In some cases this attitude reflects the enduring influence of the psychoanalytic theory of play.

The Cognitive-Developmental Theory of Play

Piaget's cognitive-developmental theory describes the characteristics of children's thinking and the changes that take place between infancy and adolescence. Piaget's observations of his own children led him to conclude that children's intellectual development takes place in stages. The sensorimotor stage is from birth to about age two. The preoperational stage is approximately between ages two and seven. The concrete operational stage is approximately between ages seven and eleven. The formal operational stage is from approximately age eleven onward. Detailed descriptions of the distinguishing characteristics of each stage are found in most child development and introductory psychology textbooks. Piaget's cognitive-developmental theory has been extremely influential. It stimulated a great deal of research and it became the rationale for many of the practices of care providers and teachers.

Several years after the publication of his cognitive-developmental theory, Piaget published his theory of play. Piaget identified three stages of play: practice play, symbolic play, and games with rules. These three stages of play correspond to the sensorimotor, preoperational, and concrete operational stages of cognitive development (see Table 2.1). Rubin, Fein, and Vandenberg (1983) have noted that Piaget's stages of play appeared in earlier publications by C. Buhler in 1928 and H. Spencer in 1873.

Table 2.1

Piaget's Stages of Play

Stages of Play	Characteristics of Play	Cognitive Development	Approximate Ages
Practice play	Behavior repeated for its own sake	Sensorimotor stage	0–2
Symbolic play	Pretending Make-believe	Preoperational stage	2–7
Games with rules	Social obligation Cooperation Reasoning	Concrete operational stage	7–11
(No further stage)		Formal operational stage	11–adult

"Practice play" is the term Piaget used to describe some of the behaviors of infants. When an infant repeats a behavior for its own sake, Piaget would classify it as play. The infant derives pleasure from the sense of control associated with practice play. The playful repetition consolidates the infant's mastery of the behavior.

In symbolic play a child lets one thing stand for something else. The child is pretending or involved in make-believe. The pretending child is, through play, organizing his or her life experiences.

In order to play games with rules, children require a sense of social obligation and the ability to cooperate and reason. These are characteristics of children at the concrete operational stage of intellectual development.

Box 2.2
Piaget's Research Methods

Piaget's book *Play, Dreams and Imitation in Childhood* is the English translation of *La Formation du Symbole Chez L'enfant: Imitation, Jeu et Rêve; Image et Représentation*, published in 1945. Piaget's theory of play is derived primarily from his observations of his own three children. This was the third book based on Piaget's study of his children Jacqueline (b. 1925), Lucienne (b. 1927), and Laurent (b. 1931). In 1936 he had published the French edition of *The Origins of Intelligence in Children* and in 1937 he had published the French edition of *The Construction of Reality in the Child*. Piaget developed his theoretical perspectives on infancy and play from his study of just three children.

Some commentators have been skeptical of Piaget's findings because of his small sample, the lack of objectivity in a parent's observations of his children, and the fact that he did not use standardized testing procedures. In other words, Piaget has been criticized for his decision to use naturalistic and informal methods to study children rather than experimental methods derived from the natural sciences. Piaget's response to these criticisms of his methods was that cognitive structures are "too complex to be revealed by less flexible standardized research techniques" (Brainerd, 1978, p. 41).

Ginsburg and Opper (1979) point out some of the advantages associated with Piaget's study of his own children. They argue that his intimate relationship with his subjects "allowed him to *discover* phenomena which might have gone unobserved or unnoticed in the laboratory" (p. 28). Ginsburg and Opper also see Piaget's familiarity with his subjects as enabling him to more accurately interpret their behavior.

Piaget's theory of play continues to exert a very strong influence on attitudes and practices. Although Piaget's theory of play just describes the stages he observed in his own children (see Box 2.2), it has been interpreted as prescribing what ought to be for all children. Piaget described the years from two to seven as the stage of symbolic play during which children's play includes pretending and make-believe. Many in the field of child care believe children in that age bracket *should* be involved in make-believe play. For example, to earn an "excellent" rating on the Harms and Clifford (1980) *Early Childhood Environment Rating Scale*, a child care facility must have a variety of dramatic play props related to various themes, it must provide adequate space for dramatic play, and it must use pictures, stories, and trips to enrich dramatic play (p. 29). Similarly, Piaget described the years from seven to eleven as the stage of games with rules. This has been interpreted to mean children in that age bracket *should* play games with rules. For example, the National Association of Elementary School Principals (1993) identifies quality indicators in school-age child care programs; one is the availability of a variety of activities, including indoor and outdoor sports and games (p. 18). The merits of deriving curriculum objectives from developmental theories are currently being debated within the child care profession.

Although Piaget's original research is read by relatively few, brief summaries of the highlights of his work are commonplace. In the area of play, his most significant contribution has not been the identification of the stages of play. Rather, his enduring influence has come from his linking of play and intellectual development. By identifying stages of play that are parallel to stages of cognitive development, Piaget increased the respectability of play. Educators, parents, and care providers agree on the goal of promoting children's intellectual development. Thanks to Piaget and those who have paraphrased and spread his message, play is seen as a way of supporting children's intellectual development. If cognitive development is worthwhile and if play and cognitive development are intertwined, the status of play is greatly enhanced. Play can be justified as a way of promoting learning and toys can be marketed for their educational value.

The Behavioral Theory of Play

Behavioral theory describes the effects of reinforcement on an organism's behavior. From the behavioral perspective, play is seen as a learned behavior shaped by positive and negative reinforcers in the child's environment. The behavioral analysis of play focuses on the observable. An understanding of behavioral theory is essential for care providers. Although it does not provide a comprehensive explanation of children's play, it does alert care providers to the powerful impact they can have on children's play. For good or for ill, consciously or unconsciously, care providers reinforce some play behaviors and discourage others. The behavioral theory of play has stimulated care providers to be aware that their own behavior is a significant element in the play environment. Having been sensitized to their potential to influence children's play, care providers are obliged to learn how to do so in ways that are beneficial to the children. It is somewhat ironic that the behavioral theory of play, with its focus on observable behaviors, is the theory that causes care providers to remember that when they are with children they are in the ethical domain. Care providers are in a position to affect children's welfare. Since care providers cannot avoid reinforcing some behaviors, a commitment to ethical practice includes doing so in a way that promotes the children's well-being.

Reinforcement can be a very effective means of influencing children's behavior. Adults who work with children are in a position to use behavioral techniques to encourage behaviors they value and discourage other behaviors. Care providers should be aware of which play behaviors they value and reinforce and which play behaviors they try to discourage or extinguish. Each care provider should identify and scrutinize the play behaviors in each category. Reinforcement can be either helpful or harmful to children. It can be used either as a way to support their growth and development or as a means of discouraging play that is beneficial. Care providers can reflect on their use of reinforcement by asking themselves: Do the play behaviors I reinforce support children's healthy growth and development in all domains? Is my reinforcement of play behaviors respectful of the individual profiles of the children in my care? Do I use reinforcement techniques to exercise control or to manipulate children in ways that are not in their best interest?

◆ ◆ ◆ ◆ # Criticisms of the Theories of Play

There is widespread dissatisfaction with the main theories of play that have been put forward. Care providers point out that they are "not useful in practice" (Monighan-Nourot, Scales, & Van Hoorn, 1987, p. 10). The theories are criticized by Sutton-Smith for presenting a "middle-class, sanitized view of children's play [while ignoring] the darker, more hostile and aggressive sides of peer play" (Vandenberg, 1986, p. 9). Kelly-Byrne (1989) has looked at the theories of play from a feminist perspective and found them to reveal "sexist biases and tacit male assumptions" (p. 250). Specifically, she criticizes the emphasis they place on defining the structure of play while ignoring children and relationships "as active agents in the construction of experience and knowledge" (p. 250). Post's (1978) review of the literature critical of Piaget's theory of play concluded that the theory is incomplete, with "omissions of data, inconsistencies within the system, and concepts which are not supported by experimental evidence" (p. 41). None of the commentators has a positive thing to say about the present state of theory building. There have been other theorists who have broadened our thinking about play (summarized by Rubin, Fein, and Vandenberg, 1983), but they have had almost no influence on child care practice.

✦ ✦ ✦ ✦ A Challenge to Care Providers

The absence of a well-regarded theory of play to guide care providers presents an opportunity and a challenge. Academics from the various disciplines that have shown an interest in play cannot be expected to provide care providers with a useful theoretical framework. They are restricted by the perspectives of their own disciplines. Care providers, however, collectively have a wealth of experience working with children, watching them play, and participating in their play. Care providers are sensitive to the whole child and know from experience that play is a complex, multifaceted activity. The time has come for care providers to propose new, third-generation theories of play that reflect the understandings derived from their work with children.

The three second-generation theories of play emphasized different aspects of children's play: play as a means of expressing emotions, play as a reflection of intellectual development, and play as a response to environmental influences. Care providers may find aspects of all these theories to be helpful. In addition, the theories that care providers develop might emphasize additional aspects of play that reflect their own perspectives. For example:

◆ play as a child's way of pursuing happiness

◆ play as a medium for connecting with others

◆ play as a way of understanding oneself

◆ play as a means of integrating development

The lack of an established, widely agreed-upon theory of play allows care providers to bring new, creative perspectives to theory building, without any restricting assumptions. In this process, care providers should not assume that there is a single "true" theory of play to be discovered and adopted by all. There may be many very helpful theoretical perspectives. All of these ideas, including those that are still incomplete and evolving, can be shared at staff meetings, at conferences, and in newsletters. Together, care providers can sift them, combine them, and add to them. The combined insights and experiences of child care practitioners represent the most likely source of the theories of play that will guide the care providers of the twenty-first century. In the future, researchers may work in partnership with front-line care providers to empirically test the new theories.

◆ ◆ ◆ ◆ # Chapter 2 in a Nutshell

The following major understandings were introduced in Chapter 2:

◆ There is at present no strong, comprehensive, widely accepted theory of play.

◆ Before 1930, four theories of play were influential: the surplus energy theory, the recreation theory, the instinct theory, and the recapitulation theory.

◆ The second-generation of play theories—the psychoanalytic theory of play, the cognitive-developmental theory of play, and the behavioral theory of play—have been dominant since the 1930s.

◆ Contemporary play experts are critical of the second-generation theories of play.

◆ Care providers are encouraged to become involved in theory building and put forward theories of play that reflect their own experiences and perspectives.

At Practicum

1. Observe your sponsor care provider's behavior when children are involved in pretend play. Does your sponsor usually participate in the play? Or does your sponsor usually keep out of the play and observe from the sidelines?

2. At your practicum placement, look for examples of adults reinforcing play behaviors. Record in your notebook some of the children's play behaviors that were reinforced and the techniques the adults used to reinforce them.

3. Ask your sponsor to share with you some of the important things about children's play that he or she has learned from working with children.

Extend Your Learning

1. If you have access to a college library, find a journal article that describes an experiment designed to learn more about children's play. What theory of play did the researcher use as the starting point for this experiment?

2. Observe a child's play for at least 30 minutes. Do not become involved in the play. Describe the play. How might that play have contributed to the child's intellectual development?

3. Based on your own childhood experiences and your informal observations of children, develop a first draft of your own theory of play. Show your draft to a classmate. Ask your classmate to help you refine and polish your theory of play. Help your classmate to refine and polish his or her theory of play. Discuss with your classmate the practice implications of your theories. In other words, if a care provider accepted your theories of play, what might he or she do when working with children?

Look Inward

If you are using this book as a textbook for a course, you will not be asked to share your answers to these questions with your instructor or classmates. These questions are provided to stimulate introspection.

1. Recall two or three adults who cared for you when you were a child. What were their attitudes toward your play? Did they treat it as important or as a waste of time or as something to keep you out of their hair for a while? Did they participate in your play? What attitudes did those care providers pass on to you?

2. Does the psychoanalytic theory of play ring true for you? Do you think your own make-believe play helped you to work through and gain control of your emotions? Do you recall expressing your emotions in your play?

3. Recall a recent situation in which you were part of a child's play environment. It may be a situation with your own child, a situation at practicum, or any other situation involving you and a child at play.

   a. Recall your behavior. What did you say or do that an observer would consider to be reinforcement?

   b. What behaviors on the child's part did you reinforce?

   c. In retrospect, was your use of reinforcement ethical? In other words, was it in the child's best interest and did it promote the child's well-being?

3
Supporting Play in Inclusive Programs

Objectives

◆ to identify some of the benefits of inclusive child care

◆ to discuss the attitudes, skills, and knowledge needed by care providers in inclusive programs

◆ to propose ways in which care providers can overcome resistance to inclusiveness

◆ to discuss the value of good communication between the care provider and parents in inclusive play environments

◆ to identify ways in which administrators can support inclusiveness

What Is Inclusive Child Care?

The NAEYC definition of developmental appropriateness (Bredekamp, 1987) consists of two parts: age appropriateness and individual appropriateness. Knowledge of a child's age is a starting point, but care providers need much more information in order to plan developmentally appropriate play experiences. They also need to know the unique characteristics of the individual children in their care. A developmentally appropriate play environment reflects the care provider's understanding of individual children's unique "growth patterns, strengths, interests, and experiences" (Bredekamp, 1987, p. 3). Sensitivity to the unique profile of each child is at the foundation of inclusive child care.

Inclusive child care programs accept any of the community's children who are in the age bracket served by the program. Children are not denied admission because they are different in some way. Children who are unable to engage in all of the usual program activities are not excluded. They are welcomed and encouraged to participate according to their individual abilities. The care providers support all children and facilitate their involvement in the program.

Inclusive Play

Inclusive play programs are essentially individually appropriate programs. The care providers plan play experiences that match the children, whatever their backgrounds or unique characteristics. All of the children in the group have the necessary time, space, access to toys and other props, and adult support and encouragement to play. The play is chosen by the children and is an end in itself. It is not therapy. It is not used as what Fewell and Kaminski (1988) call "an intervention" (p. 155). It is not academic training in disguise. It is not a contrived means of attaining objectives specified in a child's Individual Education Program. It is definitely not used "as a reward or privilege for good work" (Wehman, 1978, p. 279) or denied to children as punishment. Each child's play will be unique. It may or may not resemble the play of the majority of the children's age mates. Inclusive care providers accept these individual differences and provide play environments that suit children's developmental characteristics and prior experiences.

Inclusive programs take whatever steps are necessary to support the play of all children. For example, if a child uses a wheelchair, the care providers ensure that the shelves where playthings are stored are accessible, that the facility is barrier-free, and that the activity choices always include options that this child can access. The care providers modify the environment in whatever ways are necessary to allow that child to participate in the program and choose his or her play activities. When the care providers plan special events such as outings, they check the destinations in advance to be sure they are accessible and can be enjoyed from a wheelchair. In their day-to-day program planning, the care providers provide play opportunities that support all domains of the child's development (see Box 3.1).

Box 3.1
Supporting the Whole Child

Children with disabilities, health problems, and atypical developmental profiles should not be thought of just in terms of their exceptionality. Care providers should approach them as they would approach any child, sensitive to the importance of their development in all domains. For example, a child who is blind needs opportunities to develop physically, emotionally, socially, cognitively, and morally. The play experiences created for this child will accommodate the fact that he or she is blind. They will also support the broad goal of facilitating development of the whole child.

◆ ◆ ◆ ◆ The Benefits of Inclusive Child Care

Inclusive child care is advocated because it is both practical and morally right. Inclusive child care programs give all of the community's children opportunities to play. Choosing, exploring, and using playthings alone and with other children are important experiences for all children. Supporting the play of all children, without regard for the extent to which they resemble or differ from the majority of children in the community, has many benefits.

Benefits to Children

In a review of the research literature, Guralnick (1990) found that exceptional children benefit from participating in inclusive early childhood programs. Inclusive child care for all age groups helps all children to reach their potential. Inclusive child care programs allow children to meet and play with a diverse group of peers. Children learn from these experiences and contacts that everyone is unique and that differences are not a barrier to playing together and becoming friends. Children who participate in inclusive child care programs see adults modeling acceptance and respect for diversity. They have the opportunity to learn positive attitudes that will make their community a better, more humane place in which to live.

Benefits to Families

The need for child care services is not limited to families with children displaying the typical developmental profile. The Roeher Institute (1993) has pointed out that families need support and temporary relief services in order to avoid institutionalizing children with disabilities. Child care services are an example of this support. Inclusive child care provides the context for parents to become acquainted. Parenting is always a challenging responsibility and it is made even more difficult when parents feel isolated. Connections with other parents can result in friendships and mutual support. The parents of children whose development is atypical, parents who are new to the community, and parents in stressful circumstances face additional challenges. These parents, in particular, need the friendship of other parents in the community.

Benefits to the Community

Every community is made up of people with a wide range of experiences, cultures, lifestyles, abilities, talents, aptitudes, medical needs, and temperaments. It is in the best interest of the community as a whole to recognize and celebrate that diversity. Most North American communities do not have a tradition of acceptance, let alone celebration, of differences. Our record, unfortunately, has been one of exclusion of some community members. Lack of acceptance has impoverished community life. Communities have been missing out on contributions that could be made by the excluded individuals. Inclusiveness causes us to address issues such as our responsibilities to one another and the values we wish to see reflected in our communities. Inclusive communities demonstrate to the world a commitment to the values of mutual respect, mutual support, and caring for one another.

Moral Considerations

Inclusiveness is consistent with the highest moral principles identified in Gilligan's (1982) model: compassion, and in Kohlberg's (1975) model: justice, equality, and respect for the dignity of individuals.

Preparing Care Providers for Inclusive Programs

It is not possible to point to a single body of information that will help care providers to implement inclusive play programs. Existing training programs for care providers planning careers as specialists with exceptional children rest on a small and weak research base (McCollum and McCartan, 1988). In other words, no one is sure about how best to prepare students to work in inclusive child care settings, either as generalists or as specialists.

The quest for a single ideal knowledge base may be futile. While one might study dozens of disabilities, disorders, impairments, and handicaps, that knowledge does not prepare care providers to support the play of a specific child. There is no single "best" approach for all of the children diagnosed as having the same condition. Choate (1993) has emphasized to teachers the importance of recognizing that exceptional students are a heterogeneous group in which each individual has unique learning needs. This observation is equally valid for children in child care settings.

Attitudes of Care Providers

To effectively support children's play in inclusive settings, care providers require a particular set of attitudes. In addition to acceptance of diversity and respect for individuals, attitudes they share with all care providers, those who work in inclusive programs require other characteristics:

◆ **A willingness to learn:** Supporting children's play is seen as a learning experience. The care provider learns about each child's interests and play preferences and how to most effectively support the child's play. The care provider learns how to modify the environment or the activities to facilitate each child's play. Within the context of relationships with the children, the care provider learns how to enable each child to play. The care provider expects to learn and improve his or her practice and become more effective in supporting the play of each child. The care provider recognizes that at the beginning of each new caring relationship there will be a lot to learn. The care provider is willing to learn effective ways of working with each child, learning from the children's parents and as a research practitioner.

◆ **Tolerance of uncertainty:** Care providers begin caring for each child feeling uncertain about how to create a good play environment for that child. No workshop or book can teach the care provider in advance exactly what sort of play environment is most appropriate for that particular child. The care provider must be comfortable with that uncertainty. The uncertainty decreases over time as the care provider undertakes his or her own research to discover effective ways of supporting the child's play.

◆ **Self-assurance:** A care provider enters a relationship with each child with a lot to learn and with uncertainty about how best to support that child's play. However, the care provider has confidence that his or her child care knowledge, skills, and ethics provide an adequate framework for making decisions about this child's play environment. The care provider feels that he or she will be successful supporting this child's play. The care provider knows it will be challenging, but is undaunted.

Specific Skills and Knowledge

Although the attitudes of care providers are at the center of inclusive programs, specific skills and knowledge may also be required. Care providers may need to acquire skills such as positioning and handling some children, the operation of equipment used by some children, and alternative methods of communication. Health care workers, social service workers, and others familiar with individual children can teach care providers any skills needed to successfully include those children. The particular skills needed by the care providers will be specifically for individual children. The acquisition of skills tailored to the profiles of individual children is more appropriately part of a care provider's in-service education. Generic pre-service courses on atypical child development are no substitute for child-specific in-service skills training, although they can provide a foundation of general principles and strategies.

The parents of exceptional children are usually the best source of information about their children. The parents can often give care providers a great deal of information about their children's abilities and preferences. They may have practical suggestions to help care providers adapt the environment for their children. If their children have been diagnosed as having particular medical conditions, the parents may lend the care providers pamphlets or books on those conditions to help them to understand and work with the children.

Support groups and service organizations are another excellent source of information about specific conditions or diseases. For example, informative brochures are distributed by diabetes associations to assist teachers, care providers, and others who work with children with diabetes. When care providers learn that a child diagnosed with a particular condition will be attending their program, it is worth finding out if a support group exists. The reference librarian at the local public library can assist care providers seeking information about local, regional, and national organizations of this type. Children's hospitals are another valuable source of information, providing public information packages on some medical conditions. They are also able to direct people to other sources of information such as newsletters and to local support services.

Care providers may wish to learn about family backgrounds in order to provide individually appropriate care for some children. For example, if a child whose family has recently arrived from another country comes into the facility, the care providers can better support that child if they learn about the family's culture. The care providers might read about the country and find out about the way of life there. They might contact community members from that country to learn some words and phrases in the child's mother tongue. They might make inquiries to locate translation services in order to communicate with the child's family.

◆ ◆ ◆ ◆ Working to Overcome Resistance to Inclusiveness

Policies of inclusiveness and administrative support are necessary for the delivery of individually appropriate child care. However, they are not, by themselves, sufficient to fully integrate all children. Full integration and acceptance of all of the community's children may require a shift in attitude on the part of some community members. The tradition of exclusion continues to influence the attitudes of many adults. There are still, unfortunately, strong prejudices against people who are exceptional in some ways, against people from different cultural backgrounds, and against some immigrant groups. These attitudes may reflect fear stemming from inexperience with diverse groups of people. Whatever their roots, these negative attitudes can result in pressures on care providers to abandon their policies of inclusiveness. For example, some parents may express concern that the presence of a child with a physical disability will reduce the quality of care for their own children. Other parents may not want their children to play with and form friendships with children from backgrounds different from their own.

Some of the negative attitudes expressed by parents can be overcome. For example, care providers might invite those concerned about the inclusion of a child with a physical disability to visit the facility and see that staffing levels are adequate to provide quality care for the child with the disability and for the other children. The care providers might explain the benefits associated with introducing children to people with disabilities.

It is not possible to overcome all of the negative attitudes or concerns that parents may express regarding inclusiveness. Attitudes are not easily changed. Some parents may choose not to send their children to inclusive programs. Some parents may use the child care services of inclusive programs without endorsing the policy. At home they may teach their children attitudes that hamper the full integration and acceptance of all of the children in the facility. They may direct their children not to play with certain children in the group.

Even when parents have not taught their children their own biases, but have demonstrated respect for diversity, their children may still be unsure of how to play with peers whose appearance or behavior is unfamiliar. Care providers can support acceptance of the unfamiliar child by modeling behaviors such as greeting the child, playing with or near that child, and talking to the child in a friendly way. They can also directly teach children ways of playing with the unfamiliar child. For example, a care provider might facilitate play with a blind child by telling the other children: "Emma likes to use the playdough, but she can't see the cookie cutters and playdough. It helps her if we put them where she can reach them and tell her where they are. She can't see things we are making with playdough. We can tell her what we are making and ask her if she would like to touch the things we have made."

Our play objectives for children must be developed on a child-by-child basis. Some children may remain onlookers. Some may always engage in solitary play. Some may not develop friendships with their peers. The creation of heterogeneous groups does not mean all of the children will become skilled players or popular group members. Inclusive, individually appropriate child care has many advantages. It is not, however, a quick fix for the legacy of exclusion and prejudice in our communities. It is one small but necessary step in improving the moral tone of community life.

Partnerships with Parents

Care providers have professional responsibilities to the children in their care and to the children's parents. These responsibilities to parents are highlighted in the codes of ethics developed by care providers' associations. For example, the NAEYC Code of Ethical Conduct (Feeney & Kipnis, 1989) includes an entire section, with seven ideals and eleven principles, relating to ethical responsibilities to families. The care provider's obligations to parents are widely acknowledged, and professional education programs for care providers typically include courses on the topic of working with families.

A significant component of the care provider's job involves communicating with the parents of the children. Communications between the care provider and parents can sometimes be stressful for both parties. In spite of the stress, care providers need to establish good working relationships with the parents of all of the children. Good working relationships with the parents of exceptional children are particularly valuable.

Children's parents are usually the people who have the best understanding of the children. Parents are the best source of information regarding the unique characteristics of their children. In most cases parents can describe the strengths, interests, and preferences of their children and provide other details that enable care providers to plan individually appropriate play experiences.

When a care provider meets with parents, the following suggestions may facilitate the development of productive, mutually satisfying relationships:

◆ Approach all parents with respect and courtesy.

◆ Recognize that some parents will feel anxious meeting with care providers. Some parents feel guilty using child care. Many feel insecure about their parenting and may fear that care providers, as experts in child care, will be critical of their parenting. Try to put parents at ease, but accept the fact that they may be tense.

◆ Recognize that parenting is a difficult task. It is probably the most challenging responsibility adults assume. Parents need empathy, support, encouragement, and recognition for their efforts. By addressing parents' needs, care providers are indirectly supporting the well-being of the children.

◆ Support the parent-child relationship. Avoid communicating to parents any sense of competition for the child's affection.

◆ Let the parents know you as a person, not just as a task-focused professional. Reveal your personal qualities, your warmth and caring, your patience and sense of humor. Let them know that you do not have all of the answers and that you too make mistakes.

◆ Communicate to parents a sense of teamwork, with the parents as the team captains. They have the decision-making authority. The care provider's role is to support the parents in meeting their responsibilities to their children.

◆ Be sensitive to the fact that parents of exceptional children may already be dealing with medical personnel, therapists, social workers, and teachers. Depending on the intrusiveness, quality of service, and bureaucratic systems associated with these contacts, the parents may be reluctant or skeptical about entering relationships with care providers. Do not interpret lack of trust on the part of parents as a personal rejection. The parents may simply be experiencing "systems fatigue" based on unsatisfactory dealings with the various service delivery systems.

◆ ◆ ◆ ◆ Administering Inclusive Programs

Administrators play an important role in determining the success of inclusive child care programs. They are in a position to exercise leadership in creating an attitude of acceptance of diversity. Their commitment to inclusiveness will affect the attitudes of staff and the ability of staff to serve all of the community's children (see Box 3.2).

Administrators can support inclusiveness in these ways:

◆ **Modeling:** Administrators should demonstrate respect, acceptance, and caring for all children.

◆ **Provision of in-service training:** Front-line care providers may need additional information and skills training to work effectively with some children. The program administrators should ensure that staff are adequately prepared to care for all of the children in the facility.

◆ **Reasonable adult-child ratios:** Some children require a great deal of adult support in order to participate in child care programs. Some children require the full-time support of their own specialist attendants. Others can participate in child care programs successfully if their care providers have responsibility for fewer children than usual. Each situation should be assessed to determine the level of staffing that is reasonable for the particular mix of children. Administrators should ensure that ratios allow for the provision of individually appropriate care.

◆ **Staff support:** Even though care providers may accept the principle of inclusive child care, they may lack confidence in their ability to work with exceptional children, non-English-speaking children, or children from cultural backgrounds with which the care providers have had little or no contact. Support from administrators can help care providers to learn new skills and develop the expertise needed to work with all of the children in their care. This support may take various forms: release time to attend workshops or consult with other professionals; increased budgets to allow for specialized equipment; salaries that reflect the demands of the job; sufficient time off to prevent burnout and relieve stress; and recognition for doing a difficult job well.

Box 3.2
Inclusiveness and HIV

Many child care facilities have already confronted the question of whether or not to admit children who are HIV-positive. The facilities that have not yet been asked to admit HIV-positive children will sooner or later be called on to do so. The responses to requests to admit these children reveal the extent of the profession's commitment to inclusiveness.

The question of admitting children who are HIV-positive is clearly in the ethical domain. It is an example of the most difficult type of ethical problem—an ethical dilemma. While a run-of-the-mill ethical problem requires us to identify a single relevant ethical principle and use it for guidance, an ethical dilemma involves two or more ethical principles. We are forced to choose one principle over the other or others. This is always challenging. There is no easy way of deciding which principle deserves primacy. Each of us does this on the basis of our individual beliefs and values. Having made our choices, we must then accept the consequences, for there are always negative consequences flowing from the dilemma.

At least two professional ethical principles are relevant when we consider the question of admitting children who are HIV-positive. The following principles can guide care providers:

- ◆ Care providers demonstrate caring for all children.
- ◆ Care providers promote the health and well-being of all children.

The dilemma here stems from the fact that care providers feel they ought to *both* demonstrate caring for the HIV-positive children and promote the health and well-being of the other children by protect-

continued

ing them from HIV. If care providers give "caring for all children" primacy, they might decide to admit the HIV-positive children. If they give "promoting the health and well-being of all children" primacy, they might decide not to admit the HIV-positive children. Either way, they end up violating a professional ethical principle.

Care providers have made different decisions when confronted with this dilemma. Those who have chosen to accept and care for HIV-positive children recognize the obligation to promote the health of the other children in their care. Child care facilities that include HIV-positive children usually implement the following practices:

- ◆ The HIV-positive children are not identified. Staff and parents are informed that the facility has a policy of inclusiveness but they are not told which children are HIV-positive.
- ◆ Staff receive in-service education on the subject of HIV.
- ◆ Parents are welcome to participate in the education programs.
- ◆ With all children, staff use practices that prevent the spread of HIV. For example, disposable gloves are worn when dealing with the body fluids of all children.
- ◆ Children are taught behaviors that minimize the risk of exposure to the body fluids of all other children.
- ◆ Staffing levels are adequate to ensure supervision and prompt adult response to situations that could put children at risk.

It is noteworthy that many child care facilities are implementing these practices with or without a policy of including HIV-positive children. The publicity given to the rejection some HIV-positive children have experienced in schools and child care facilities has led many parents of HIV-positive children to keep the information secret in order to protect their children from the hostility of some community members. It is reasonable to assume that some care providers are working with HIV-positive children without anyone in the facility knowing that the children are HIV-positive. The parents may have purposely withheld the information from the administrators of the facility. Other cases may simply be undiagnosed.

Administrators can also play a significant role in raising the issue of inclusiveness with administrators of other community services and agencies. Administrators of child care programs can take a leadership role in advocating policies supportive of inclusiveness throughout the community. For example, they might approach public transit officials to call for wheelchair-accessible buses. They might contact the public library to recommend the acquisition of children's books printed in Braille. They might support local events that showcase the various cultural groups in the community. Administrators of inclusive child care programs are in a position to encourage other community services to support their efforts to create an inclusive community.

◆ ◆ ◆ ◆ Chapter 3 in a Nutshell

The following major understandings were introduced in Chapter 3:

◆ Sensitivity to the uniqueness of individual children underlies inclusive child care.

◆ Inclusive programs welcome all of the community's children in the age brackets they serve and take whatever steps are necessary to support their play.

◆ Inclusive programs have practical advantages for children, families, and the community.

◆ Care providers in inclusive child care settings require a particular set of attitudes: a willingness to learn, tolerance of uncertainty, and self-assurance.

◆ Child-specific skills and knowledge may be required by care providers in inclusive programs.

◆ Care providers can model behaviors that will facilitate acceptance of unfamiliar or exceptional children and can teach children specific ways of playing with them.

◆ Good communication with parents allows care providers to acquire some of the information needed for inclusive programs.

◆ Inclusive programs require the support of administrators.

At Practicum

1. To what extent is your practicum placement inclusive of all children in the age groups it serves? Write a paragraph in which you describe your practicum placement in terms of its inclusiveness and demonstrated respect for diversity.

2. Ask your sponsor if his or her child care education was adequate preparation for the provision of individually appropriate inclusive care. Ask your sponsor to identify any gaps between his or her preservice and in-service education and the knowledge and skills needed to provide inclusive care. Note any gaps reported by your sponsor.

3. Observe the free play of a child whose development has differed from that of his or her peer group. Make a list of that child's interests, strengths, play preferences, and sources of happiness and satisfaction. How might a care provider work with that child to enhance the benefits the child derives from play?

Extend Your Learning

1. Interview a parent of an exceptional child. If possible, select an individual you know well, such as a friend or relative who will feel comfortable speaking with you. Assure your interviewee that you will protect the family's privacy and you will not use real names in your report. Ask the parent to describe his or her experiences obtaining child care for the exceptional child. If the parent agrees, tape the interview. If the parent does not want to be taped, make notes. Later, write a summary of that parent's story. Remember to protect the family's confidentiality by using fictitious names. Make minor changes to the story if the true version would make it possible for readers to identify the family. Show your interviewee your first draft of the story. Ask if it is accurate, except for the intentional changes that were made in the interest of confidentiality. Make any changes indicated by the parent. What does this parent's story reveal about your community's values? Are you proud of what this story reveals?

2. Research the administrative structure that is in place to support inclusive child care in your province, territory, or state. What legislation is in place? How is the service paid for? What do parents of exceptional children have to do to access child care? What are the pros and cons of the existing system?

3. What courses and workshops are available in your community for care providers interested in increasing their skills and knowledge related to inclusive child care? Where in your community could care providers informally obtain information that would enable them to better serve children and families who have recently come from another country?

◆ ◆ ◆ ◆ Look Inward

If you are using this book as a textbook for a course, you will not be asked to share your answers to these questions with your instructor or classmates. These questions are provided to stimulate introspection.

1. Exceptional children are sometimes spoken of as having "special needs." For example, a preschooler with Fetal Alcohol Syndrome may be unable to comprehend danger. From a special needs perspective, that child is said to need a well-supervised play environment in which particular attention is paid to safety. The special needs paradigm has been criticized by Freeman and Gray (1989) as stigmatizing and oppressive. Rather than using the term "special needs," some care providers speak of making the play environment individually appropriate. They would say an individually appropriate environment for the preschoooler with Fetal Alcohol Syndrome is well-supervised and safe. The difference between the two ways of thinking about the child is subtle. Which way of discussing and approaching exceptional children do you feel is better?

2. Although parents are the primary decision-makers for their own children, care providers are not just puppets of the parents. Productive working relationships with parents require mutual respect, not one-sided deference. Care providers must consider parents' requests and suggestions in light of their own personal and professional ethics and standards of practice. They are not able to please all of the parents all of the time. When working with the parents of exceptional children, care providers often feel great empathy for the parents and try extra hard to please them, recognizing the challenges they face. In so doing, care providers must be aware of their limits, the points at which they must say no. Reflect on your own limits. Think of some parental requests or suggestions to which you would not agree. What reasons would you give to explain your positions on those issues?

3. Recall your own childhood play experiences. Did you have opportunities to play with a diverse group of children? What attitudes toward exceptional children did your parents, teachers, and other adults teach you? What attitudes toward exceptional children do you plan to teach the children with whom you work?

4

Locally Appropriate Programs

◆ ◆ ◆ ◆ Objectives

- ◆ to define locally appropriate programs

- ◆ to describe the benefits of locally appropriate programs

- ◆ to introduce examples of local appropriateness

- ◆ to provide suggestions for care providers wishing to create locally appropriate programs

What Is a Locally Appropriate Program?

Given the great variation from community to community, it is unreasonable to expect or encourage uniformity among child care programs. A program in the downtown area of a large North American city will differ and ought to differ significantly from a program in a small hamlet in the Northwest Territories in Canada.

The various instruments and checklists designed to assess the quality of child care focus on features that leaders in the profession consider to be valid in all settings. The rating scales developed by Harms and Clifford (1980, 1989) and Harms, Cryer, and Clifford (1990) and the Canadian Child Care Federation's (1994) statement on quality child care summarize the profession's standards of practice. They identify features that the authors believe are common to all good programs. For example, Harms and Clifford (1980) advocate that all programs for preschoolers provide space, time, props, and encouragement for children's dramatic play.

Locally appropriate child care programs include the indicators of quality identified in these and other publications, but, in addition, they reflect the uniqueness of the communities they serve. They fit the setting and the children, their families, and their community. As a result, care providers cannot turn to a textbook for the answer to the question, "What props should I provide to encourage dramatic play among my four-year-olds?" The list of props that is appropriate for Community A may be inappropriate for Community B. Many items will be appropriate in both communities, but some items will be specific to one community. For example, locally appropriate props in a child care facility in a grain-farming community would include toy tractors and other farm equipment, a cardboard grain elevator, and caps like those worn by local farmers and grain elevator employees. Locally appropriate props in a child care facility in a community in which forestry is the main industry would include toy logging trucks and other logging equipment, along with ear protectors and hard hats like those worn by loggers.

A locally appropriate child care program does not exclude the distant or remote or foreign. To advocate inclusion of local content is not to reject in any way curriculum themes, materials, or activities that introduce children to new and unfamiliar topics. Certainly there is a place for such topics. Television, computers, books, and magazines have expanded children's horizons and made them aware of the whole universe. By following their lead and building on their interests, a care provider will naturally incorporate a wide variety of topics. A locally appropriate program ensures that the local people, the immediate environment, and the enriching, relevant, direct experiences available in the community are not overlooked.

A locally appropriate child care program meets the highest standards of quality, but it is not a carbon copy of any other program. While standardization of the product is considered desirable in the manufacturing and fast-food industries, it is not desirable in child care. Child care occurs within interpersonal relationships—relationships between individual care providers and individual children. Each relationship is unique and dynamic. Programs are created for specific groups of children and each program is unique. Child care is a relationship-based activity that strives to be individually appropriate. It is the antithesis of copying a prototype. In some businesses "quality control" is synonymous with ensuring sameness and uniformity. In child care, however, excellence involves taking into account the unique features of the children and the community and developing a custom-made program.

For the child care professional, making a commitment to locally appropriate practice adds an interesting and creative dimension to program planning. It means the care provider will look to the community when setting goals, selecting curriculum themes, and identifying places to visit and guests to invite. It means strengthening the partnership with parents to ensure that their ideas are reflected in the program. It means familiarizing the children with their surroundings, drawing on the many elements that make up their community. It involves introducing children to the natural world and its seasonal changes (see Box 4.1). A locally appropriate child care program also connects children with their heritage and introduces them to community life and its daily activities. Parents and other community members feel involved and respected for their contributions. In summary, the child care program is an integral part of the community, drawing from it and contributing to its social and cultural life.

◆ ◆ ◆ ◆ The Benefits of a Locally Appropriate Program

The involvement of parents and other community members in a child
care program affirms their knowledge and skills. It creates cross-gener-
ational links. It establishes bonds of shared experiences and familiarity.
It connects children with their roots. It also helps to balance the over-
whelming influence of the mass culture—the powerful and frequently
anti-social messages directed at children through television and video
games. A locally appropriate child care program also counteracts the
loneliness and isolation that characterize the lives of many citizens.

Locally appropriate child care is also a means of increasing the
continuity between families and the program. "Continuity" is the term
used in the child care literature to describe the fit between the goals
and the priorities of families and the goals and priorities of the child
care services they use. Continuity between child care programs and
families is beneficial for children. Their self-esteem and confidence are
thought to benefit when the programs are continuous with other
aspects of their lives. Powell (1994) explains that the continuity issue is
usually addressed by means of parent education, with a poor fit being
seen as an indication that parents need to be educated by the care
providers. A locally appropriate program supports continuity between
the families and the child care program, but the families are not seen as
mere recipients of education. Rather, the families are recognized as

important sources of knowledge. The assumption is that parents and care providers will share knowledge with one another and that both groups will teach and learn from one another. In other words, continuity is increased by means of collaboration and dialogue.

A locally appropriate program will probably not lead to more, better, more advanced, or more creative play. It will not speed up children's development or give them an academic advantage over children in other programs. A locally appropriate child care program will, however, provide children with ideas and "content" for their paintings, block play, and make-believe. This play will not be "superior" to the play of children whose care providers do not emphasize local appropriateness, but it will help to achieve a different goal.

Local appropriateness is advocated as a means of helping to develop healthy communities—communities that are satisfying, enjoyable places in which to live. Local appropriateness begins with the assumption that children will enjoy exploring and discovering their community. Certainly they will learn, but the cognitive outcomes are not the only reason for a locally appropriate program. By making your program an integral part of the community, you will be helping the children know and understand their surroundings. You will be raising the profile of children and encouraging adults to consider the needs of children in their decision making. You will be introducing children to a broad range of adults who have a lot to contribute. You will be demonstrating respect for diversity—diverse age groups, from teenagers to senior citizens, as well as people from diverse backgrounds and with diverse careers and interests. Overall, you will be contributing to feelings of connectedness and belonging for all who participate. Child care programs have the potential to serve as the catalyst for building healthier communities, thereby indirectly benefiting the children involved in the programs.

◆ ◆ ◆ ◆ Communities Are Unique

Your community has many characteristics that distinguish it from other communities. Geographers have identified five ways in which a community can be described: physical, spatial, human, cultural, and social elements.

The physical elements are the natural features of your community. Examples of physical elements include the climate, landforms (such as hills, marshes, lakes, and creeks), the soil, plants, and animals. All of these physical elements contribute to your community's distinctiveness.

The spatial elements pertain to the size, shape, and location of your community. The spatial elements greatly influence life in your community and make it unlike any other community.

The human elements include all of the ways in which populations may differ from community to community. These include population density, age composition, sex composition, educational status, occupational status, economic status, and cultural origins of the residents. The unique human elements in each community define its personality.

The cultural elements include all of the buildings and other facilities people have added to the community. For example, homes, schools, places of worship, libraries, parks, transportation facilities, commercial and industrial buildings, and government buildings such as post offices and police stations—all these make up a community's cultural elements. These structures contribute to the character of your community.

The social elements of your community include the population's interests and activities. The beliefs and attitudes of the residents, the traditions, the patterns of family life, the ways in which people make a living, and the level of participation in civic affairs are among the social elements that make your community unique.

◆ ◆ ◆ ◆ **Reaching out to the Community**

The first step in creating a locally appropriate program is to get to know your community. Become familiar with its physical, spatial, human, cultural, and social elements. Make lists of the features of your community in each of those five categories. Use the "Communities Are Unique" section of this chapter to help you develop your lists.

Use your lists to plan outings and to identify possible visitors to your child care facility. As you plan outings, remember that places you have seen many times may be unfamiliar to the children in your care. Also, the same site can be visited several times as you focus children's attention on different features or on seasonal changes. Similarly, repeat visits by guests are valuable. Over time the visitors will become more familiar to the children and relationships may develop.

Extend the children's understanding of the community by providing books, toys, and other props that relate to the outings and the information shared by visitors. Reinforce their learning by using the new vocabulary associated with the outings or used by the visitors. In order to help deepen children's understanding of their community, help them discover connections between the familiar and the unfamiliar, between different features of the community, and between different people and places.

There are countless ways to reach out to the community in a child care program. They can be classified into activities that involve taking the children out and activities that involve bringing people into your facility (see Box 4.2).

Box 4.2
Publicizing Your Program

Community newspapers are usually eager to include photographs and stories with human interest. Your local newspaper may be willing to publish pictures and articles relating to some of the field trips you arrange for the children and some of the visitors who come to your facility. Notify your local newspaper from time to time and inform the reporters prior to special outings or visits from community members. These activities have human interest and the reporters may decide to cover them. The children will enjoy seeing pictures of themselves in the newspaper, and community members will learn about your locally appropriate program.

When new families enter your program, inform them of the possibility that reporters may take photographs of the children and use them in human interest news stories. Ask if the parents have any concerns about their children's photographs appearing in the newspaper. If any parents are reluctant, for any reason, to have their children photographed, note this preference and ensure that those children are not photographed by reporters.

Outings

If you work in a child care center, you may need to divide the children into small groups for some outings. The destinations listed here represent a small fraction of the possibilities. The outings you choose will depend on the numbers and ages of the children in your care, available transportation, and the resources in your community. Every location has many interesting possibilities for outings.

◆ Neighborhood walks to look at, count, classify, talk about, or listen for whatever your neighborhood contains. For example: people riding bicycles, people pushing baby carriages, people driving snowmobiles, neighborhood watch signs, buses, joggers, and seasonal changes.

◆ Visits to prearranged destinations. For example: homes and gardens of neighbors, places where parents work, farms, public buildings, senior citizens' centers, and local businesses such as florists or bakeries.

◆ Field trips to local places of interest. For example: parks, museums, beaches, walking trails, landmarks, bus depots, community gardens, marinas, and public sculpture and other public art.

Visitors

Visitors to the facility will add richness to your program. The children, the guests, and the community as a whole benefit. The children gain knowledge of their community and its residents; the visitors enjoy being with and helping the children; and the community is made stronger as interpersonal connections are formed. Your visitors may also become more aware of the children's interests and needs. Each adult visitor is a potential ally when issues affecting the well-being of children are debated in the community.

◆ Invite parents, grandparents, and other adults to tell or read stories they heard when they were children, teach the children songs or games they learned when they were children, tell the children how they celebrate or observe special holidays, help the children make snacks they enjoyed when they were children, show the children interesting items and demonstrate their use or explain their significance, share information about hobbies, or tell the children about their work.

◆ Arrange social events such as potluck meals, barbecues, or picnics and invite parents, siblings, and neighbors to participate.

◆ Make arrangements with your neighborhood high school for teenagers to become involved in your program. Teenage volunteers may, under your supervision, become big buddies who read to the children or play with them.

◆ Invite families and friends to participate in observing holidays and festivals.

◆ Invite the people who come to your facility on business, such as repair people, meter readers, delivery people, public health inspectors, and fire safety inspectors to tell the children about their jobs and show them their tools or equipment.

Reflecting the Community in Your Facility

Each locally appropriate child care facility has a distinctive appearance. It is not a copy of any other facility. It may incorporate ideas borrowed from other settings, but it is also unique in many ways. For example:

◆ The facility's book collection includes children's books by local authors and illustrators, books with themes of local interest, and stories that reflect the children's heritage.

◆ The children learn songs and rhymes from the cultural groups that make up the community. The children are introduced to musical instruments that reflect their heritage and they hear music by local musicians.

◆ The playthings include locally made replicas of things that are part of the community, such as ferries in a coastal community or snowmobiles in a northern community.

◆ The coloring and facial features of the dolls resemble the people of the community.

◆ The dress-up clothes and props available to the children include items that are worn locally and items of local interest. For example, in a community in which hockey is popular, dress-up clothes would include child-size hockey pads, sweaters, and helmets.

◆ Special community events are incorporated into the curriculum. For example, if the community has an annual celebration such as a winter festival, harvest celebration, or cultural event, that theme is reflected in the child care program during that period.

◆ Much of the curriculum content is drawn from the local community. The topics and themes planned by the care provider help children learn about their community (see Box 4.3).

◆ The decor of the offices and other adult spaces reflects the community in which the facility is located. For example, the work of local artists is displayed. The space is decorated with attractive local materials such as dried wildflowers.

Box 4.3
Care Providers as Curriculum Developers

Much of the planned curriculum of a locally appropriate child care program is informed by the community in which the program is situated. The notion of local appropriateness is at odds with the assumption that a single excellent program can be developed and packaged and plugged in anywhere.

Care providers in locally appropriate child care programs are actively involved in curriculum development. They set goals, select content, and choose the methodologies that suit specific communities, families, and children. Care providers in locally appropriate programs do much more than implement a standardized off-the-shelf program. They consult with community members. Working as research practitioners, they assess and refine their programs. They exercise professional judgment and apply professional expertise to develop programs that enhance the quality of community life.

◆ ◆ ◆ ◆ Reflecting Community Values

Locally appropriate child care programs are respectful of the goals and values of the families they serve. In order to reflect the community's values, care providers need to become aware of local views and priorities. Care providers who are long-term members of the community in which they work may already be aware of local perspectives on child care issues. Care providers who are new to their community need to learn what local people consider important.

Clarifying the Community's Views

To bring the community's views into your program, you will need to consult with parents, grandparents, and other community members who have an interest in services for children and families. A neighborhood or community child care advisory group is a good starting point for gathering the information you will need. If your community does not have an advisory group, you may decide to organize one by inviting interested community members to come together to discuss child care issues. If the people you approach are too busy to get together as a group, you may be able to consult with them individually to find out what the community's child care priorities are. For example, in some communities, there may be an interest in promoting bilingualism and biculturalism within the context of child care. In some communities, parents may want a child care program that helps their children learn to speak English well. In some communities, parents may want child care that emphasizes preparation for or reinforcement of the elementary school program. Each community will have its own particular values and priorities.

In some communities, families prefer to let the care provider establish the goals of the program. When this happens, it may be possible to learn their views by asking for their reactions to the program. Create opportunities for community members to provide feedback on an ongoing basis. If they are aware that you are open to their opinions, you may eventually be able to involve them more in determining the appropriateness of your program. You can also learn about the community's values by observation. Notice how parents and others respond to the initiatives you take to make the program locally appropriate. Listen to their comments after an outing or a visit by a community member. Watch for their reactions when they see local books, music, playthings, and dress-up clothes in the facility. Notice how they respond to locally appropriate curriculum content. These informal reactions reveal the values of community members just as well as formal philosophy statements developed by advisory groups and boards of directors.

When Values Conflict

In the course of developing and implementing a locally appropriate child care program, the care provider is likely to encounter differences of opinion. Community members may have diverse views on child care issues. The views of community members may conflict with those of the care provider or with the views of experts in the field of child care.

If members of a community child care advisory board disagree regarding goals or policies, there are various ways of handling the disagreement. The board members may decide to vote on the issue in question and adopt the majority position or discussions may continue until consensus is reached. A decision may be arrived at that includes some elements of the positions advocated by all board members.

Once the community's child care values and preferences are known to the care provider, as a result of either formal policy statements made by an advisory group or informal consultations and observations, the care provider may find that those values are at odds with his or her own values or with those of child care experts. In such a situation, the care provider must analyze the significance of the conflict. If the care provider concludes that the issue has consequences for the children's well-being and that the community's values on the topic in question ought to be seriously considered, he or she needs to choose a course of action. The action chosen will depend on factors such as:

◆ whether accepting the community's views on this matter would violate accepted standards of child care practice or any of the care provider's personal or professional ethics;

◆ whether the accepted child care practice is reasonable, supported by research, and generalizable to this community;

◆ whether the community's position was reached after considering its consequences and with an awareness of alternatives;

◆ whether compromise is possible.

Depending on the answers to these questions, the care provider might decide to:

◆ accept the community's position;

◆ facilitate an open discussion and re-evaluation of the matter with community representatives, identifying alternatives, considering relevant research on the topic, and identifying probable consequences of accepting each alternative;

◆ as a research practitioner, plan a trial of each of the conflicting approaches to learn the consequences of each, then share the results with community representatives and reconsider the matter;

◆ take a firm, principled stand on the issue, providing community members with a clear explanation of his or her position and the principle at stake.

Each situation involving a conflict between the care provider's values and the community's child care values presents a learning opportunity. The care provider may learn useful new perspectives from community members. Value conflicts cause the care provider to reflect on his or her values and ethics, resulting in increased self-knowledge. Conflicts may stimulate fruitful discussions with community members and may lead to research within the child care facility in order to learn more about the topic under discussion.

When Differences Are Irreconcilable

Locally appropriate child care programs have many advantages. However, local appropriateness is not an ultimate value, one that takes precedence over all others in child care settings. For example, after a full and open discussion of the topic, parents and other community members in Community Z might endorse a policy of spanking children as a means of influencing their behavior. Spanking might be advocated by several religious leaders in Community Z and approved by a majority of the adults. In Community Z, spanking is widely believed to be an appropriate child guidance technique. Spanking may violate the personal and professional ethics of a care provider working in Community Z. The care provider should not violate his or her ethics for the sake of local appropriateness. In a case of conflict, ensuring the well-being of the children is a higher order principle than reflecting community values. In this case, if the members of Community Z insist that the care provider use spanking, the care provider should take a principled stand and refuse. If the community members make acceptance of their policy a condition of employment, the appropriate response on the part of the care provider is to resign.

◆ ◆ ◆ ◆ Play in Locally Appropriate Programs

The play of children in locally appropriate programs has not been studied by researchers or contrasted with the play of children in other programs. Care providers working as research practitioners can make a significant contribution to our understanding of the impact of locally appropriate programs on children's play. By actively observing the children in their programs, care providers can answer questions such as these: Do children spontaneously build into their dramatic and sociodramatic play roles and themes based on community members they have met? What percentage of children's play themes comes from television and what percentage is drawn from their own experiences in the community? Are the playthings that replicate things found in the community more or less popular than other playthings?

◆ ◆ ◆ ◆ Looking to the Future

The possibility of pursuing community enhancement goals in tandem with the provision of child care services is being investigated in the developing world (Landers, 1991). This approach is just beginning to be explored in the North American context. For example, some First Nations communities are developing locally appropriate child care services that involve Elders and parents and that reflect their cultures, traditions, and value systems (McCallum, 1995; van Raalte, 1995). Community enhancement is being approached from a broader perspective than economic development. Healthy communities are seen as more than prosperous economic units. Locally appropriate child care programs are serving as a starting point for more encompassing community development work. Although this work is in its early stages, the approach appears to hold promise. The two-way connections between child care programs and families, neighborhoods, and communities seem to offer many potential benefits for the children and for the communities.

If the concept of local appropriateness is accepted by care providers, we can expect to see an increase in the diversity of North American child care programs. Increased diversity is also predicted by Spodek (1991) in his discussion of the criteria that ought to be the basis for choosing the content of the early childhood programs. He argues that "there is a real possibility that no one curriculum will be acceptable to all and that no one true concept of development will be established" (p. 16). Although Spodek's position is not framed in terms of local appropriateness, he points out that there any many conceptions of knowledge and many conceptions of development. The next step seems to be to reflect these differences in programs for children by developing locally appropriate child care.

◆ ◆ ◆ ◆ Chapter 4 in a Nutshell

The following major understandings were introduced in Chapter 4:

◆ Locally appropriate programs reflect the children, their families, and the community.

◆ A locally appropriate program introduces children to their community and creates links among community members.

◆ Locally appropriate programs are advocated as a means of enhancing the quality of communities.

◆ Care providers in locally appropriate programs exercise creativity and professional skill as curriculum developers.

◆ Care providers can learn the views and priorities of local families and other interested community members through consultation.

◆ Community members may have diverse opinions and values.

◆ If local appropriateness is endorsed by care providers, the diversity among child care programs will increase.

◆ ◆ ◆ ◆ At Practicum

1. Ask your sponsor what policies are in place and what procedures are followed when children are taken on outings and field trips. Find out how children are transported, how costs are covered, and how the children's safety is assured while they are away from the child care facility.

2. To what extent are community members involved in this child care program? Are visitors from the community a regular or rare part of the program? List any visitors or parents you have observed contributing to the program since the beginning of your practicum.

3. Ask your sponsor how the child care facility communicates with parents and other community members. What methods does your sponsor think are most effective in eliciting the views of the parents and other community members? What methods does your sponsor think are most effective in providing parents and others with information about the program?

◆ ◆ ◆ ◆ Extend Your Learning

1. Obtain a map of your community. Mark the locations of places of interest that care providers might choose as field trip destinations.

2. Visit your local public library. Ask the librarian to recommend some books on the history of your community. Scan one of the books and make notes of local historical events that you think school-age children would find interesting.

3. Begin to develop an address book containing the names and phone numbers of local people you might call on to participate in your own child care program someday. Beside each name list the contribution that individual might make.

◆ ◆ ◆ ◆ Look Inward

If you are using this book as a textbook for a course, you will not be asked to share your answers to these questions with your instructor or classmates. These questions are provided to stimulate introspection.

1. In this chapter, locally appropriate child care programs are described as helping to balance the influences of the mass culture—particularly the anti-social messages contained in television and video games. Do you agree or disagree with this assessment of the messages children receive from television and video games? In your opinion, is there any need to balance the influences of the mass culture? If so, do you think it is even possible to balance the influences of the mass culture?

2. Do you believe care providers should attempt to deal with issues that are beyond the direct care and education of children—issues such as the quality of community life or the isolation and loneliness of community members? Should those broader problems be left to others such as social workers or politicians? Should child care professionals remain focused on child care? How would you defend your position if someone asked your opinion?

3. Care providers in locally appropriate programs must be aware of their own values and ethics. They must be able to express their own views when issues are being discussed with parents and other community members. They need to be clear about the issues on which they would be unwilling to change or compromise. What would be your reaction if you were working in a child care center and the parents advocated the following policies?

   ◆ Staff should use "time-out" to enforce rules of conduct.

   ◆ The free play period should be reduced by half.

   ◆ Staff should follow the program outlined in the new book *The Ideal Preschool Program.*

   How would you state your own views on these issues?

Supporting the Play of Infants and Toddlers

5

◆ ◆ ◆ ◆ ◆ Objectives

◆ to outline prevalent perspectives on the development of infants and toddlers

◆ to describe good play environments for infants and toddlers

◆ to identify personal qualities of care providers who support the play of infants and toddlers

The Development of Infants and Toddlers

Child development theorists and researchers have identified various aspects, or domains, of development. The NAEYC definition of developmental appropriateness (Bredekamp, 1987) includes four domains: physical, emotional, social, and cognitive. Moral development is variously classified as a separate, fifth domain or as an aspect of social development or cognitive development (Windmiller, Lambert, & Turiel, 1980). Some families and religious leaders speak of and nurture a sixth domain—spiritual development. This domain is usually not addressed in the child development literature or in textbooks for care providers in training. Although children's spiritual development is most often omitted from child development publications, it is important to many parents. Care providers need to be aware that parents' views on child raising may reflect their beliefs regarding the best ways to promote their children's spiritual development.

Although child development theorists and researchers often focus on a single domain, care providers are responsible for the development of the whole child. In addition, the NAEYC encourages care providers to practice in ways that are individually appropriate—that is, taking into account each child's "growth patterns, strengths, interests, and experiences" (Bredekamp, 1987, p. 3). The task of caring for and educating infants and toddlers involves the application of a great deal of knowledge. Your child development courses will provide you with much of that essential information. The intent here is to briefly summarize some of the aspects of development relevant to the planning of play experiences for infants and toddlers.

Physical Development

Between birth and their third birthdays, children change from tiny, totally dependent creatures characterized by a few reflex behaviors to running, climbing, talking, throwing, building, chasing, scribbling, playing preschoolers who are able to perform countless physical tasks. The rapid rate of growth and skill acquisition between birth and age three is unparalleled. Planning for the play of infants and toddlers involves taking into account each child's large- and small-muscle control, eye-hand coordination, balance, mobility, and strength. Play needs to provide opportunities for infants and toddlers to use their present physical abilities while leading the way to the next milestone. For this reason, care providers should know the sequence of the milestones that characterize normal physical development.

The physical abilities of infants and toddlers determine the types of play they will enjoy. Care providers should approach each child as a unique individual. The published descriptions of the ages at which infants and toddlers usually reach each milestone of physical development are of limited value to care providers planning play experiences for *particular* infants and toddlers. Knowing that the majority of babies between the ages of three months and six months attempt to reach and grasp objects does not help a care provider play with a specific three-month-old, although this knowledge may help the care provider decide appropriate times to introduce new play experiences. The best sources of information regarding the physical development of an infant are the care provider's observations and experiences playing with that infant.

Emotional Development

Erikson (1950) articulated a theory of personality development that he entitled "Eight Ages of Man." Erikson saw each of the eight stages between infancy and maturity as involving a major developmental crisis. He described the eight crises as a series of alternatives. Since the alternatives involve feelings, Erikson's model has been interpreted as representing stages of emotional development. The developmental crisis of infancy, according to Erikson, is Basic Trust vs. Basic Mistrust. The developmental crisis of the second year is Autonomy vs. Shame and Doubt. Although Erikson stated that he did not intend his stages to be "a prescription to abide by . . . in the practice of child-training . . . or in the methodology of child study" (p. 270), care providers have been strongly influenced by this theory. Many practices in the care and education of infants and toddlers are advocated or defended in terms of the need to build trust or promote autonomy. Care providers who accept Erikson's theory plan play experiences for infants and toddlers so as to help them become first trusting and then autonomous.

Erikson's theory has received a lot of attention, and summaries of the crises are found in most child development textbooks and handbooks for parents. Erikson's theory began as a description of stages of human development, but it is now interpreted by many as prescribing how children's emotional development ought to occur. Many adults assume that infants need to learn to trust and toddlers need to become autonomous.

Erikson's model is just a theory, and care providers should approach it critically. Its validity should not be assumed. Care providers should test it against their own observations of infants and toddlers. Working as research practitioners, care providers are in an ideal position to observe children's emotional development and determine whether Erikson's model accurately describes the children in their care.

Erikson's model is not value-neutral or culture-free. The emphasis on autonomy reinforces the cultural values of independence and self-reliance. Although these values are widely held in North America, they are not held by everyone. Some groups, including some First Nations and some women's organizations, value cooperation, interdependence, and mutualistic approaches to human relationships. It is unreasonable to conclude that children raised in environments that are less enthusiastic about autonomy are destined to feel shame and doubt.

Erikson's model focuses our attention on a single personality attribute in each stage. This appears to oversimplify the emotional life of infants and toddlers. During infancy and toddlerhood much more is happening in the emotional domain than the options presented in the "crises" Erikson identified. Babies and toddlers demonstrate a wide range of emotions. By framing emotional development in terms of pairs of alternatives, Erikson may have restricted our perspectives on the emotions of infants and toddlers. The existence of the stages and nature of the stages should be questioned by care providers.

Social Development

The social development of infants and toddlers is intertwined with their emotional development. Infants and toddlers need to form bonds with caring, nurturing adults. These relationships are essential to children. Warm, caring relationships give infants and toddlers the security they need to tackle other developmental challenges. When we play with infants and toddlers we are involved in relationship building. By interacting with babies playfully and by engaging toddlers in play, care providers are communicating messages such as: *I care about you; I enjoy being with you; you're wonderful.* Caring relationships with their significant adults add joy to children's lives. This experience of joy within relationships is a base for all later social development.

Interactions between infants and toddlers in groups are not classified as friendships. Friendships based on proximity are thought to begin at about age three. Children's friendships are discussed in more detail in Chapter 8. Infants and toddlers do show an interest in one another and watch one another. Toddlers display a range of behaviors toward peers. Research by Wanda Bronson cited by Garvey (1990) found that nearly half of the encounters between one-year-olds ranged from mild to distressful disagreements or struggles (p. 34). Bronson found that one-year-olds prefer toys over peers. Although Dunn (1993) reports that toddlers sometimes display "understanding of and a sensitivity to the feelings and intentions of others" (p. 59), such behaviors do not represent typical toddler interactions. Their play is most often solitary.

Cognitive Development

Piaget's theory of cognitive development places infants in what he called the sensorimotor stage and two-year-olds at the beginning of the preoperational stage. During the sensorimotor stage, babies learn about their environments by using their senses. Around age two children enter the preoperational stage. They are acquiring language and beginning to use symbols to represent objects or events.

Piaget also pointed out that infants and toddlers pass through a number of substages. At each substage, children's thinking structures are qualitatively different. The differences between substages are not just a matter of the children knowing more. At each substage, according to Piaget, children interpret information differently. Their ways of thinking and understanding change as they move from one substage to the next. Planning for the play of infants and toddlers involves taking into account their ways of thinking. They do not think abstractly or in ways that are logical to adults. For example, young infants do not understand what Piaget called "object permanence"—that objects exist when they are out of the baby's sight (see Box 5.1).

Box 5.1
Object Permanence

The aspect of Piaget's study of infants that has attracted the most interest has been his description of how children develop the concept of object permanence.

Before the age of four months his children made no attempts to search visually or to retrieve objects that disappeared from their view. After the age of four months they began to show first signs of object permanence. They would look on the floor for things they happened to drop and they would look for vanished objects in the last places they were seen. However, they did not actively search for hidden objects by lifting a cloth or pillow.

Piaget observed that between the ages of 9 months and 12 months his children began to search for hidden objects. At this stage Piaget found this searching pattern: He would hide an object at point A. The child would search for it and find it. He would hide the object at point B while the child watched. The child would search for it at point A.

Between the ages of 12 months and 18 months the children began to search for hidden objects differently. They would search in the last place they saw the object disappear. Piaget would hide an object at point A. The child would search for it and find it. He would hide the object at point B while the child watched. The child searched for it at point B.

Between the ages of 18 months and 24 months Piaget observed another change in his children's ability to find hidden objects. At this stage they were able to find objects even when they did not observe them being hidden. For example, Jacqueline watched Piaget put a coin in his hand, then put his hand under a cover. He withdrew his closed hand. She opened his hand and then searched under the cover for the coin. He would then take the coin back, put it in his hand, and slip his closed hand under a cushion. She would immediately search for it under the cushion.

Piaget's perspective on cognitive development has been very influential. Although subsequent research has raised questions about some features of his theory, it continues to dominate the early childhood field. Indeed, the tasks Piaget used with his own children when he was developing his perspectives on the development of infants and toddlers are used by some care providers as learning activities for infants (Honig and Lally, 1981).

Piaget's descriptions of cognitive development should be viewed with the healthy skepticism accorded to all theories. Care providers as research practitioners can, as Piaget did, observe and note the changes that take place in the thinking of infants and toddlers. They can then apply that knowledge to provide the children with play experiences that match their abilities.

Alternative Perspectives on Development

This brief overview identifies some of the ways in which the development of infants and toddlers can be described. This outline is far from complete. It includes only European–North American cultural perspectives on infants and toddlers. These perspectives have high profiles in the publications found in North American libraries. There are other informative perspectives on the development of infants and toddlers that can assist care providers in their work.

North American adults see children from a variety of perspectives and they hold differing views regarding the characteristics of a "good" child and the ways adults should interact with children. The perspective outlined above—focusing on the physical, emotional, social, and cognitive domains and the theories of writers such as Erikson and Piaget—is familiar to people who have studied psychology. However, it should not be assumed that this perspective is necessarily better or more insightful than other perspectives. Families and communities view the development of infants and toddlers in many different ways, sometimes influenced by their religious beliefs and cultural traditions, and sometimes influenced by parenting books and magazine articles they have read. Care providers encounter these varied perspectives in their work with families.

Most alternative perspectives on the development of infants and toddlers are not published. They are part of the pool of wisdom and insights to be found within individual communities. Creating a locally appropriate program may involve finding out about how people in the community think about childhood and child development. This knowledge may be accessible through the parents of the children in your care. More likely, it will rest with the grandparents and other community elders. Seek out these local perspectives. You may find in your own backyard a theory or several theories of child development more useful to care providers than the patchwork quilt of single domains, armchair theories, expert opinion, and research available in libraries. Families have been caring for and educating infants and toddlers since the beginning of human history. Information about infant and toddler development has been passed from generation to generation within families and communities. Accessing that information will deepen your understanding of infants and toddlers and enable you to create a program that reflects local perspectives.

The theories of infant and toddler development, both published theories and theories found in the oral traditions of families and communities, can give care providers useful perspectives on children. Awareness of theories prepares care providers to notice things that they might otherwise overlook. The theories also provide frameworks for interpreting children's behavior. All of these ways of looking at infants and toddlers deserve to be considered carefully and critically. The notion of developmental domains is part of current child care orthodoxy, and many people speak and write about children using that language. This approach has limitations, however. It is the product of a particular time, place, culture, and set of values. The unpublished theories that are part of the oral traditions of families or communities deserve comparable scrutiny and attention to their underlying values. Their merits and usefulness are yet to be determined. The unpublished theories are worth discovering and evaluating. It may be that the child care profession has unintentionally been ignoring important and useful perspectives on children.

◆ ◆ ◆ ◆ Play Environments for Infants and Toddlers

Play environments include physical and social elements. The room arrangement, furnishings, equipment, decorations, and toys are features of the physical environment. The social elements include the people—the children, the care providers and other staff, parents, and other visitors to the facility. The relationships among these people create a social atmosphere that affects play. A good play environment has a relaxed, friendly, respectful atmosphere and a mood of harmony.

The creation of a suitable physical environment for infants and toddlers is a large part of the care provider's job. The creation of a good social atmosphere and the development of positive adult-to-adult relationships are just as important. Relationships among staff members influence the atmosphere in a child care facility. Personality conflicts and differences in values and ethics must not be allowed to negatively affect the play environment. Managers must be sensitive to the importance of adult-to-adult relationships within the facility. New personnel should be selected with attention to the need for harmonious staff relationships. Managers are responsible for the equitable treatment of staff; perceived disparities in workloads or privileges can destroy staff harmony. Good working relationships among the adults, on the other hand, can create a more relaxed atmosphere for children and model cooperation and mutual support.

Play Environments for Babies

Most babies spend a great amount of time sleeping in the first few weeks of life. When they are awake, their interactions with care providers revolve around the routines of feeding, burping, diapering, bathing, and changing clothes. Between these routines there are usually visits from admiring friends and relatives eager to meet and hold them. Very young babies are growing and gaining strength, forming attachments with people around them, and sensing their surroundings. The people in babies' lives are the most significant components of their play environments. Care providers create excellent play environments when they take a playful approach to babies, performing the routine tasks in an upbeat, cheerful, playful way—making up games, using a pleasant voice, humming or singing to soothe them, and showing babies through smiles and funny faces that it's fun to be with them. Playful care providers communicate to babies that their company is enjoyed, and that routine activities are opportunities for pleasant visits and interesting games.

As the weeks pass, babies spend more of their time awake. Provided the floor is safe, warm, and draft-free, babies can spend their awake periods on a blanket on the floor. Otherwise, a playpen is preferable. They actively look at the people and objects around them. As they gain control of their eye muscles they are able to follow moving objects. Good play environments for these slightly older babies include interesting things for the babies to look at. For example, there are mobiles above their cribs, they have mirrors, pictures, and other objects to look at during the routines of diapering and dressing. The care providers play games that encourage babies to actively look. They bring toys and other items within the babies' range of vision, moving the objects slowly so the babies can follow them with their eyes. As with all age groups, the play environment is more than just the objects and the activities. The relationships between the care providers and the babies are the leading quality indicator. High-quality relationships are evident in a playful, gentle tone during these games and cheerful conversations with the babies about the items being looked at. Both the babies and the care providers enjoy the interactions.

As babies reach each of the physical and cognitive milestones of infancy (such as gaining control of their hands, crawling, understanding the effects of their actions, and understanding object permanence), the play possibilities expand greatly. Care providers remain central to the play environment, but babies are increasingly interested in and able to explore the space and objects around them. Care providers continue to playfully perform the routine tasks, but as babies acquire physical skills their care providers are no longer the only source of entertainment and fun. The role of the care providers shifts slightly as they must now create safe, interesting spaces in which infants can play and explore and practice their growing repertoire of skills. Taking babies on outings allows them to experience all sorts of new sights and sounds. By acting as tour guides on outings, naming the things the babies are seeing, hearing, feeling, or smelling, care providers enhance babies' enjoyment. These older, increasingly competent infants reward adults with their smiles and laughter and mastery of new skills when care providers sit on the floor and play with them. Beside them on the floor is the perfect place to talk about their toys and other playthings, name things in picture books, assist with large-muscle activities, or play games with them. Playing with infants on the floor, a care provider can see them developing new physical skills, enjoying the adult-child relationship, and developing new thinking structures (see Box 5.2).

Box 5.2
Treasure Baskets

Elinor Goldschmied and Sonia Jackson (1994) suggest that babies who are able to sit independently be given "Treasure Baskets" to explore. In their book *People under Three: Young Children in Day Care*, they discuss the value of Treasure Baskets. A Treasure Basket is a flat-bottomed basket about 5 inches (13 cm) high and at least 14 inches (35 cm) in diameter. It is strong enough to support an infant leaning on it. Goldschmied and Jackson specify that it should not be made of plastic as they prefer natural materials.

The Treasure Basket in their illustrations is made of woven wicker. The Treasure Basket is filled with objects of different textures, smells, tastes, sounds, and colors, and shapes. Again, they specify that the objects should not be plastic. The Treasure Basket is placed on the floor beside the seated baby and the baby chooses items to explore. Goldschmied and Jackson list over 90 objects that are suitable for a baby's Treasure Basket. It is noteworthy that none of the objects is a "bought toy." Most are household odds and ends. All of the objects they recommend are too large to be swallowed. The following items are included in their list:

- a piece of loofa
- a lemon
- a shaving brush
- a bamboo whistle
- clothes pegs
- a small funnel
- a bottle brush
- lengths of chain
- a velvet powder puff

Although Goldschmied and Jackson do not advocate plastic playthings, durable plastic items have the advantages of being washable and long-lasting. They can be sanitized in a dishwasher or hand-washed and rinsed in a bleach solution. Some of the objects Goldschmied and Jackson recommend for Treasure Baskets would have to be discarded and replaced after being used by a baby because they would not stand up to the necessary washing.

Play Environments for One-Year-Olds

During the second year of life, infants become increasingly mobile, first toddling around furniture and later walking alone. One-year-olds delight in physical activity—for example, climbing; putting objects into containers and dumping them out again; pushing, pulling, and carrying objects; removing objects from shelves and drawers; throwing objects; stacking objects; and splashing, scooping, and pouring water.

Good play environments allow toddlers to safely engage in these physical activities. Mobile one-year-olds need more space for exploration than they needed as babies. Care providers are still very important as sources of encouragement and assistance and conversation about the activities. However, one-year-olds are capable of spontaneous, self-initiated activity, and they will play independently, exploring their surroundings and investigating the materials they find. Leavitt and Eheart (1985) emphasize the value of providing toddlers with long blocks of time for self-directed play. They also advocate that care providers follow the children's lead as play evolves, regardless of who initiates it (p. 25) (see Box 5.3). Leavitt and Eheart caution care providers who work with toddlers to avoid using the teaching methodologies found in schools, such as lessons, artificial teacher talk, and adult-led activities.

Box 5.3
Following Their Lead

The role of care provider in children's play changes as the children gain skills and experience. The change is in the direction of the children assuming more and more control of the play. When we play with young babies, we take the lead. The games and the playful interactions are our initiatives. Before long, infants are able to choose their toys and play activities. They are able to initiate their own play and play independently. They are able to decide for themselves when they have had enough of one toy and are ready to move on to something else. They are able to decide for themselves how to use their toys and other playthings. Their ways of playing may or may not coincide with adult notions of how the items "ought" to be used. Following their lead involves acceptance of their increasing abilities and allowing them to make their own play choices and set their own pace.

continued

The care provider creates a safe, supportive play environment that includes a variety of developmentally appropriate playthings. With encouragement to explore, infants and toddlers will make choices and engage in play that is individually appropriate. When adults show respect for children's play choices, they are enhancing their relationships with the children. They are protecting the children from unnecessary stresses caused by adults imposing their own, possibly individually inappropriate, expectations on the play.

By following the children's lead, the care provider is allowing them to be active decision-makers. One of the broad, long-term goals of education in democratic societies is the preparation of children for active decision making. Choosing one's playthings and deciding how to use them are activities that start children on the long road to becoming competent decision-makers.

Play Environments for Two-Year-Olds

Two-year-olds have been described as "bustling bundles of energy, intent on exploring the world around them" (King, Oberlin, & Swank, 1993). Their physical abilities are constantly improving. They can run forward and backwards, hop, jump, dance, kick balls, toss and catch, and maintain their balance on narrow surfaces. Their small-muscle skills are sufficiently developed to allow them to scribble, use snap-together blocks, string large beads, and assemble simple puzzles. Good play environments for two-year-olds have the space and equipment needed for their large- and small-muscle activities.

Most two-year-olds want to do things themselves. They are becoming increasingly independent, feeding themselves, dressing and undressing themselves, and beginning to use the toilet or potty. In spite of this growing competence and stated desire to do things themselves, two-year-olds continue to be dependent on their care providers. They still want care providers to be nearby. Two-year-olds still need care providers' hugs and smiles, admiration for their accomplishments, back-up support when they attempt tasks that they can't yet manage themselves, and comfort when they tumble or trip in the course of their exuberant activities. Care providers are somewhat like battery chargers for two-year-olds. They come to care providers for encouragement, help, or comfort, and once recharged they return to their explorations.

Two-year-olds are beginning to enjoy dramatic play, acting out roles they have observed. The dramatic play of two-year-olds is different from the sociodramatic play of older children. In dramatic play each child's role is independent of others. In sociodramatic play two or more children assume roles related to a common theme. Props related to the children's experiences can support dramatic play. Outings and visitors will provide children with experiences that may appear in their dramatic play. For example, a bus trip may stimulate dramatic play that incorporates this theme. A care provider might provide props to encourage that play. The props need not be realistic toy replicas for the dramatic play to be enjoyable. Two-year-olds can pretend that an object represents something else. For example, stuffed animals arranged in a row can represent people sitting on the bus. A doll can represent the bus driver. An empty cup can represent the fare box.

◆ ◆ ◆ ◆ Providing a Safe Environment

Mobile infants and toddlers delight in their new skills, such as their ability to get to and examine things that attract them. Their mobility and inclination to explore, combined with their lack of awareness of danger, create the potential for accidents. Protecting the children from harm is the care provider's first responsibility (see Box 5.4). Care providers must always ensure that the play environments are hazard-free and that children are adequately supervised. Good play environments for mobile infants and toddlers encourage them to move and touch and explore. Breakable or dangerous articles are removed from the environment so that children are able to investigate without constant restrictions or admonishments not to touch. The play area is kept free of small objects that infants and toddlers could swallow or push up their noses. Since the explorations of infants involve putting everything into their mouths, all of the playthings are washed frequently and rinsed in a bleach solution.

Child care centers are usually able to provide a safe, single-purpose space designed just for the use of infants and toddlers. In family day care homes, however, it is not always possible to create a space that infants and toddlers can freely explore without restrictions. Unless there is a room dedicated just to them, it may be necessary to restrict their explorations. For example, if the mobile infant and toddler's play space is in the kitchen and living room, they cannot be allowed unrestricted freedom. By childproofing the area as much as possible—removing ornaments, placing special latches on cupboards containing anything the children should not play with, placing barriers around heaters, and so on—the need to intervene and redirect their explorations is kept to a minimum. The potential dangers inherent in a multipurpose space call for constant vigilance.

Child care settings often include children of various ages. Safe play spaces for infants and toddlers in child care centers are usually separate from the play spaces for older children, primarily out of concern for the safety of the younger children. Ensuring the safety of infants and toddlers in mixed age groups presents an additional challenge to care providers if the play space is shared, as in most family day care homes. The most practical arrangement may be to create barriers between the play areas used by the infants and toddlers and those used by older children. Many of the toys and other materials used by preschoolers cannot safely be used or explored by the infants and toddlers. The play of the older children may include constructing block structures, forts, or routes for toy vehicles. If mobile infants or toddlers are allowed access to these projects, it is likely that the structures will be knocked down, causing upset and frustration among the older children. The play activities of the older children may also put the infants and toddlers at risk of being hurt. For example, the large-muscle activities of preschoolers could result in collisions with babies or toddlers. Concentrating on their play, the older children may inadvertently bump into and frighten or injure infants or toddlers.

Box 5.4
Safety Checklists

The Canadian Child Care Federation's *National Statement on Quality Child Care* (1994) includes safety checklists for child care centers and family day care homes.

A safe center:

◆ is sanitary and free of hazards

◆ is equipped with operable safety devices

◆ is equipped with first aid supplies that are accessible indoors and outdoors and on excursions for the numbers of adults and children normally present

continued

- provides locked storage space for tools, cleaning products, medicines, etc.
- defines limits both indoors and outdoors in the interest of safety
- accommodates the physical environment of children with special needs, including ramps, handrails and physically accessible buildings
- is furnished with toys, equipment and play materials which are safe for the development level and needs of the children in attendance (p. 13)

A safe family day care home:
- permits easy exit in the event of necessary evacuation
- is clean, in good general repair and free from dangers
- is equipped with functioning safety devices, including smoke detectors, fire extinguishers, gates, electrical outlet covers
- is adequately equipped with readily available first aid supplies
- contains storage space which is inaccessible to children for tools, firearms, hazardous and combustible products, drugs and medicines and other dangerous items
- contains, or has access to, outdoor play space which is maintained in a safe condition (p. 24)

Source: Canadian Child Care Federation. (1994) National statement on quality child care. Ottawa, ON: Author.

◆ ◆ ◆ ◆ Care Providers for Infants and Toddlers

The care provider is the most influential variable in the play environment of infants and toddlers. Our attitudes toward play, our knowledge of child development, our sensitivity to the unique characteristics of each child, and the quality of the relationships we form with children will affect the play of the children in our care.

Since our attitudes toward play can have such a significant impact on our behavior, it is important for care providers in training to become introspective—to become clear about their own beliefs and values regarding play. Your beliefs and values are the product of a lifetime of experience and are part of who you are. You should do an honest assessment of your attitudes toward play—its importance in the healthy development of infants and toddlers, your feelings about being on the floor playing with children, and your goals for infants and toddlers.

Many people outside the field of child care believe play to be unimportant, that adults will spoil infants and toddlers by playing with them, and that the only worthwhile activities are educational—preparing children for the competitive, high-tech world. Your training program and this book may be introducing attitudes toward play that are new to you. Perhaps you are in a transition period between attitudes you brought into your training and new approaches that you are learning about. Perhaps the approaches you are studying are a perfect fit with the beliefs and values you acquired before you decided to become a care provider. It is essential that you know and are able to express your point of view. By putting your beliefs and values regarding play into words you will be able to stand back and look at them critically, to see if you are comfortable with them, and to look for congruence between what you profess and what you do.

As care providers, our work with infants and toddlers and our involvement in their play reflect more than our beliefs and values. Every interaction is an expression of our personalities, revealing how we feel about ourselves, how we approach life, and how we cope with challenges. In some occupations it is possible to do the job while revealing little or nothing of our personalities. In the field of child care our personalities are an integral part of the job. The essence of ourselves is on display in everything we do when we are with children.

Qualities of Care Providers

Who is likely to provide infants and toddlers with good play experiences? The personal qualities needed to provide quality care and education include the following:

◆ **The ability to show caring:** With infants and toddlers the demonstration of caring involves a lot of touching, cuddling, stroking, patting, and holding. Care providers need to be comfortable with this contact. A caring relationship is the starting point for supporting play, and with infants and toddlers that means frequent picking up, hugging, rocking, and having them sit on our laps.

◆ **Warmth:** A warm care provider approaches infants and toddlers in a relaxed, gentle way. Interactions with the children are positive and pleasant. The care provider's demeanor communicates interest in the children and willingness to meet their needs. A warm care provider smiles and maintains eye contact with babies and toddlers when "conversing" with them.

◆ **Patience:** Working with infants and toddlers requires endless patience. Care providers who are easy-going accept toddlers' wanting to do things themselves that an adult could do more quickly. They let the children set the pace.

◆ **A sense of humor:** A sense of humor and a lighthearted outlook on the part of the care provider will help children enjoy the funny side of life. Adults who are fun-loving support children's play by communicating a playful approach to the tasks at hand.

◆ **Acceptance of uniqueness:** Each infant and toddler is a unique individual with his or her own temperament and preferences. Care providers entering relationships with infants and toddlers should expect and be comfortable with individual differences.

◆ **No unresolved personal issues:** Providing care for infants and toddlers involves a lot of giving and a high degree of what Alice Honig (1990) calls "emotional availability." Adults with personal problems that restrict their ability to give of themselves will probably be unable to create optimal play environments.

Working with infants and toddlers is a special and very important vocation. It certainly is not for everyone. While the knowledge required to do the job can be learned, the personal qualities are not teachable in the same way. The introspective process must include an examination of your personality and an assessment of whether or not your qualities match the needs of infants and toddlers.

Chapter 5 in a Nutshell

The following major understandings were introduced in Chapter 5:

◆ The physical development of infants and toddlers is characterized by rapid growth and skill acquisition.

◆ Prevailing perspectives on the emotional development of infants and toddlers are dominated and restricted by Erikson's (1950) theory.

◆ Infants and toddlers benefit from warm, supportive relationships with their care providers.

◆ Piaget identified changes in the thinking of infants and toddlers, and he described the changes as a series of stages and substages.

◆ Other perspectives on child development are worth discovering and evaluating.

◆ Play environments include physical and social elements.

◆ People are the most significant part of a baby's play environment.

◆ Good play environments for mobile infants and toddlers allow them to explore and investigate.

◆ It is the responsibility of care providers to create and maintain safe play environments and provide constant supervision of infants and toddlers at play.

◆ Working with children reveals the personalities of care providers.

◆ Potential care providers should assess their own personalities in relation to the qualities needed to provide infants and toddlers with excellent care: the ability to showing caring, warmth, patience, a sense of humor, acceptance of uniqueness, and the absence of unresolved personal issues.

♦ ♦ ♦ ♦ At Practicum

1. Observe an adult engaged in the routines of care for a baby aged less than three months. Look for evidence of a playful approach to that baby. After observing, list in your notebook all of the playful behaviors the adult demonstrated.

2. Spend at least half an hour on the floor playing with an infant who is aged between 6 months and 12 months. Afterwards, list all of the physical skills the baby demonstrated.

3. Look at the toys and other playthings available to the two-year-olds in your practicum placement. Place about 10 toys and other play-things on a continuum from most popular to least popular with the two-year-olds.

◆ ◆ ◆ ◆ Extend Your Learning

1. Interview a friend or relative who is a grandparent. Ask your interviewee to share with you his or her ideas about how infants and toddlers should be cared for. Ask how infants and toddlers were cared for in the past. Ask your interviewee to advise you on the care of infants and toddlers. Write a report summarizing what you learned from this grandparent.

2. Visit a toy store or the toy department of a department store. Look at toys that are labeled as being appropriate for infants and toddlers. If you could purchase three toys for the infants and toddlers in a child care facility, which ones would you select? Explain your choices. Are any of the toys labeled as appropriate for infants and toddlers actually inappropriate? If so, name them and explain why they are inappropriate.

3. *Toddler Day Care: A Guide to Responsive Caregiving* (Leavitt & Eheart, 1985) includes an excellent appendix entitled "No-Cost or Low-Cost Materials and Equipment for the Child-Care Center." The following materials are some of the items listed in the appendix:

    ◆ large boxes, crates, and cartons   ◆ egg cartons

    ◆ milk cartons   ◆ string

    ◆ dress-up clothes   ◆ old socks

    ◆ plastic bottles   ◆ magazine pictures

    Begin collecting these materials to use in your own child care program someday. Ask your friends to begin saving these materials for you too. Leavitt and Eheart's book includes suggested uses for the dozens of materials included in their list.

Look Inward

If you are using this book as a textbook for a course, you will not be asked to share your answers to these questions with your instructor or classmates. These questions are provided to stimulate introspection.

1. Some books containing program ideas for care providers suggest activities that involve using food as a plaything. For example: stringing macaroni; using beans or rice in gluing projects or in homemade shaker toys; using wheat as a sand substitute in indoor sandboxes; making playdough with peanut butter, powdered milk, and honey. How do you react to such suggestions? Are food products acceptable playthings? If you were setting the policy for a child care facility, what would your policy be regarding the use of food in play?

2. Recall the way your grandparents, parents, aunts, and uncles approached infants and toddlers. Try to recall specific things those family members said or did that revealed their attitudes toward infants and toddlers. Use the views of one or more of your family members to write your family's theory of child development. Include the family's major assumptions and beliefs about infants and toddlers. Put check marks beside the major assumptions and beliefs that you agree with.

3. Reread the personal qualities needed by care providers who work with infants and toddlers. Do you agree or disagree with the suggestion that people with these qualities are better suited to the job than people without these qualities? Would you make any changes to the list? At this time in your life, do you think infant and toddler care is for you?

6 Supporting the Play of Preschoolers

Objectives

◆ to summarize characteristics of the development of preschoolers

◆ to discuss good play environments for preschoolers

◆ to identify professional ethical principles relevant to planning and supporting children's play

◆ ◆ ◆ ◆ The Development of Preschoolers

Between their third birthdays and the beginning of Grade 1 at approximately age six, children are in their "glory days" of play. Preschoolers love to play. Their play reflects their development, and their development promotes their play. Play is at the center of their lives. In every domain of development preschoolers are making strides that increase their play options and enhance their enjoyment of play.

Physical Development

Many of the large- and small-muscle skills that first appeared in toddlerhood are refined during the preschool years. Movements become more controlled and proficient. Coordination and balance improve. The overall quality of gross-motor activities improves along with the precision of small-motor movements. These physical changes allow preschoolers to enjoy new forms of play such as riding tricycles and other pedal vehicles, moving to music, building with smaller blocks, putting together more difficult puzzles, and engaging in more adventurous outdoor climbing and exploration. The play of preschoolers reflects their expanding physical skills.

Emotional Development

Descriptions of the emotional development of preschoolers are dominated by Erikson's (1950) perspective. His theory is widely cited, but of little practical value to care providers working with preschoolers. According to Erikson, the developmental crisis of the preschool years is Initiative vs. Guilt. Erikson used the term "initiative" to mean the ability to undertake, plan, and attack a task. The alternative to developing initiative is "guilt over the goals contemplated and the acts initiated in one's exuberant enjoyment of new locomotor and mental power" (p. 255). Erikson's discussion of this stage reflects his Freudian point of view and focuses on children's psychosexual development. Erikson interpreted the behavior of preschool boys as "phallic-intrusive" and the behavior of preschool girls as demonstrating "catching," which may involve either aggressive snatching or "making oneself attractive and endearing" (p. 255). He also described the preschool period as the stage of the "castration complex." Although Erikson's theory is very often referenced in textbooks for care providers, the summaries of the Initiative vs. Guilt stage found in many of those publications bear little resemblance to Erikson's description of the stage. For example, Hendrick (1994), Read, Gardner, and Mahler (1987), Feeney, Christensen, and Moravcik (1991) all refer to Erikson and the Initiative vs. Guilt stage, but they all apparently liked the label but not Erikson's explanation of the stage. This incongruity suggests that Erikson's perspective on the preschool years is not helpful to care providers and that his theory is at odds with the observations of those textbook authors. It seems the time has come for care providers to seek another perspective on the emotional development of preschoolers. It makes no sense to continue to promote Erikson's label for the stage while replacing his description of it.

The rejection of the position of a long-accepted authority reminds us of the need for care providers to generate new theories that fit their own observations and experiences with children.

Instead of using Erikson's theory to look at the emotional development of preschoolers, care providers might start with the observation that preschoolers experience a wide range of emotions. Preschoolers express their emotions both verbally and nonverbally, and in both socially acceptable and socially unacceptable ways. Developmentally appropriate practice with preschoolers would include helping the children to name their emotions and express them in socially acceptable, nonhurtful, nondestructive ways (see Box 6.1).

Box 6.1
Expressing Emotions

Care providers can help preschoolers name their emotions and find an acceptable way to express them. For example, if Max is angrily throwing blocks after a block structure he was building fell down, the care provider would first stop him from throwing blocks and then help him label his feelings. For example, the care provider might say, "It seems to me that you're feeling frustrated and angry because your blocks fell down." The care provider does not deny Max's feelings or communicate that those feelings are wrong or inappropriate. However, he or she should then help Max understand that throwing blocks is not an acceptable way of showing those

continued

feelings. Someone could get hit by a block and it would hurt. Anything that hurts or might hurt another person is not an acceptable way of expressing one's feelings.

The care provider would teach Max acceptable ways of behaving when he feels frustrated and angry. For example:

◆ He might tell someone, "I feel angry and frustrated. I worked hard making the tower and it fell down."

◆ He might get a big ball of playdough and pound it into a flat pancake.

◆ He might draw a picture of himself feeling angry and frustrated and ask the care provider to print "Max feels angry and frustrated" on the picture.

◆ He might use one of the musical instruments in the center and make some music expressing anger and frustration.

This proposed approach to emotional development is drawn from the child guidance literature. Helping children to name their feelings is a component of a child guidance technique known as Active Listening that is taught in Parent Effectiveness Training and Teacher Effectiveness Training programs. This approach may be more practical than the directive to foster initiative and prevent guilt.

This perspective on the emotional development of preschoolers provides an example of how research practitioners could contribute to the understanding of children. Research practitioners might ask questions such as: What emotions are experienced by the children in my care? How do the children express those emotions? How do staff react when children express emotions? How do children react when staff name the emotions the children are expressing? What socially acceptable ways of expressing emotions did the staff suggest? Does this approach seem to be helpful to the children? If not, how might it be improved? Individual care providers might answer these questions in their own facilities and then share them with friends in other facilities to compare findings. Eventually, their answers should be shared with colleagues at conferences and published in newsletters and journals read by care providers.

Social Development

During the preschool years, children seek relationships with other children. Their relationships with their adult care providers remain very important, but preschoolers are increasingly involved with their peers.

Initiating Play with Other Children

In his study of preschoolers, Durkin (1986) observed that the children experienced pleasure at being together. He concluded that the pleasure of being accepted by other children is the motive for children trying to join play groups. He interpreted preschoolers' efforts to initiate play with other children or join established play as attempts to form relationships with the other children. Although preschoolers may want to establish relationships with peers, they are unsure about how to go about it. Using trial and error, preschoolers are unsuccessful in 70% of their attempts to establish play or gain access to play.

The high rates of rejection reported in the research literature raise a question for care providers. Is it appropriate for care providers to directly teach preschoolers techniques that might increase their chances of success in establishing play with others or gaining access to play groups? Chapter 2 pointed out that many care providers are inclined to remain on the sidelines and observe children's play. Their reluctance to become involved is widespread, perhaps because of lingering influences of psychoanalytic theories or perhaps because of their desire to foster independence. The topic of teaching preschoolers ways of establishing or joining play is not addressed in the leading textbooks for care providers in training.

This question of whether or not care providers should directly teach preschoolers techniques for joining play groups or establishing play activities with other children is an example of a question that research cannot answer for us. The research literature tells us what techniques children use in the process of trial and error, and the frequency with which they use the various techniques, and the success rates associated with each technique, but it cannot answer "should" questions. Care providers must answer such questions themselves through the application of their own beliefs, values, and ethics.

It is important to recognize that individuals may make different decisions than their colleagues. For example, care providers A, B, and C may all endorse the ethical principle "Promote the well-being of all children." They may agree that adhering to that ethical principle involves practices such as fostering children's development, enhancing children's independence, and addressing their individual needs. However, they may weight those elements differently. Care provider A may believe it is extremely important to promote children's social development. The other aspects of development are important, but for Care provider A, social development takes primacy. This value placed on social development may lead Care provider A to decide to teach preschoolers the techniques that research has found to have higher success rates. Care provider B may believe it is extremely important to foster independence. Care provider B believes that children benefit from working out their own problems and finding solutions themselves. This value placed on independence may lead Care provider B to decide not to teach preschoolers the techniques that have the higher success rates, but to allow the children to figure them out independently. Care provider C may analyze this question on a case-by-case basis. In some cases, Care provider C lets children find their own solutions to problems. However, if a particular child is seen to always fail in attempts to establish play with other children, Care provider C may place that individual child's need for playmates first and directly teach that child some techniques that might produce more success.

Decisions such as this come up constantly in the practice of child care. It is essential that care providers become aware of their beliefs, values, and ethical principles because they will form the framework for their decision making.

Care providers who decide to directly teach preschoolers techniques for establishing or joining play can use as a starting point the work of Durkin (1986). Durkin's research findings have not been widely reported in child care publications. However, they constitute one of the "nuggets" mentioned in Chapter 1. His research is of interest to both practitioners and scholars. Durkin observed three- to five-year-olds in a preschool, focusing on the strategies they used in over 1400 attempts to either establish play with another child or join play groups of two or more children. He observed children using 33 different strategies to establish or join play. It is noteworthy that their overall acceptance rate was only 28.7%. In other words, using their own strategies, preschoolers fail almost three-quarters of the time in their attempts to establish play with another child or join the play of two or more children. Of the 33 strategies the children spontaneously used, the most successful one was "Variant of Ongoing Behaviour" (p. 184). This involved the preschooler entering an area where a child or children were playing and (verbally and/or nonverbally) producing behavior similar to the play of the other child or children. When the children used this strategy, they were successful in establishing or joining the play 60.7% of the time. However, the children used this strategy on less than 2% of their first attempts to establish or join play. In summary, the children wanted to establish or join play, but the strategies they used failed over 70% of the time. The strategy with the greatest success rate was very rarely used. Since even the most successful strategies failed at least 39% of the time, it appears that children need to learn to use several strategies and to deal with frequent rejection.

Durkin's findings have important implications for care providers. They provide guidance on the selection of strategies to teach children. Of the 33 strategies that Durkin (1986) observed, the following are the ones with the best success rates:

◆ **"Variant of Ongoing Behaviour.** Entering into area where episode is underway and (verbally and/or nonverbally) producing behaviour similar to that underway" (p. 184)

◆ **"Questioning Another.** Entering into area where episode is underway and verbally asking another about his/her play activity" (p. 184)

◆ **"Play Gesture.** Performing an action that is meant to indicate that a child wants to play. This action is not similar to that of the group or person being approached, i.e., it is not a variant of ongoing activity" (p. 183)

◆ **"Encirclement and Moving Closer.** Walking around person or group playing or moving closer to them" (p. 184)

Durkin's findings raise questions that care providers could pursue as research practitioners. For example: What joining and entering strategies are used by the children in my care? Which strategies are successful? Which strategies are unsuccessful? How can preschoolers be taught to use strategies that have a higher likelihood of success? Are books and other media an effective way of teaching preschoolers successful strategies for joining and entering play? Do all children eventually figure out for themselves effective strategies for joining and entering play?

Parten's Stages of Social Participation

Chapter 1 suggested that the research literature on the topic of play is largely unhelpful to care providers. One of the notable exceptions is a study published in 1932 by Mildred B. Parten. Her study of the social development of preschoolers has achieved "classic" status. The terms Parten coined to describe the stages of children's social development ("solitary play," "parallel play," and "cooperative play") are now so widely used that they often appear without references to Parten's work.

Parten observed 42 children during free play in a nursery school setting. Although she refers to these children as preschool children, her sample included 18 children younger than age three. Today these children would probably be classified as toddlers and only the three- and four-year-olds in her sample would be classified as preschoolers. Parten used her observations to develop six categories of social participation (see Table 6.1).

Table 6.1
Parten's Categories of Social Participation

Category	Description
Unoccupied behavior	The child is not playing. The child watches anything of momentary interest.
Onlooker behavior	The child watches other children play. The child often talks to the children who are playing, but does not enter the play. The child remains within speaking distance of the play group and watches and listens to the play.
Solitary independent play	The child plays alone and independently with toys that are different from those used by children playing nearby
Parallel activity	The child plays independently among other children. The child uses toys that are like those used by nearby children. The child does not try to influence or modify the activity of nearby children. The child plays beside rather than with the nearby children. There is no attempt to control the coming or going of children.
Associative play	The child plays with other children. The conversation concerns the common activity. There is borrowing and lending of play material. Children follow one another with trains or wagons. Mild attempts are made to control who may or may not play in the group. All members engage in a similar activity. There is no division of labor or organization of the activity around any material goal or product. The children do not subordinate their individual interests to that of the group. Conversations reveal the children to be primarily interested in their associations, not in their activities.
Cooperative or organized supplementary play	The child plays in a group that is organized for the purpose of making some material product, attaining some competitive goal, dramatizing situations, or playing formal games. There is a marked sense of belonging or of not belonging to the group. One or two members control the group and direct the activities of the others. There is a division of labor. Members take different roles.

Parten's categories have endured since the 1930s and they contin-ue to be useful to care providers who work with young children. According to Parten's classification system, cooperative or organized supplementary play is the most socially advanced type of play. However, Parten's classification system may be expanded to include a seventh category: empathic play. A child playing empathically makes allowances for another child and modifies the play to enhance the other child's enjoyment. For example, an older child may change the play to accommodate the abilities of a younger child, or a more skilled child may make adjustments when playing with a less skilled child. Care providers as research practitioners can provide evidence to sup-port or reject the existence of empathic play. Observations made by care providers might determine the ages at which children begin to demonstrate empathic play and the environmental factors that enhance or detract from children's ability to play empathically.

Parten's categories of social participation provide a valuable per-spective from which to observe children's play. Although the categories represent changes and the acquisition of additional social skills, Parten's stages should not be thought of as resembling an escalator moving in one direction until the child gets to the top and can engage in cooperative play. Children who are able to play cooperatively some-times choose other types of play such as solitary independent play, parallel play, or onlooker behavior. In other words, Parten's categories are not comparable with models of development that are represented by ladders or other hierarchical images.

Cognitive Development

Preschoolers are in what Piaget called the preoperational stage of cog-nitive development. The most noteworthy feature of this stage is the development of language. Throughout the preschool years children's vocabularies are expanding and they are learning the grammar of the language or languages they hear. The play of preschoolers includes conversation. They talk to themselves, to one another, and to their care providers. They also speak "in character" during their dramatic and sociodramatic play. Care providers can support children's language development by conversing with them about their play. The play pro-vides the topic of conversation. The conversations should be natural rather than mini-lectures or quizzes. When it is appropriate and nonintrusive, the care provider can chat with individual children and give them an interested audience.

This is a period of a great deal of hands-on learning for preschoolers, of active exploration to find out how things work and to discover the consequences of their own actions. The preschool years are a time of learning from first-hand experience, manipulating objects and materials, and getting to know the environment by interacting with it. In addition to learning from direct experiences, preschoolers learn from television, books, and computer programs to which they are exposed (see Box 6.2).

Box 6.2
Reading to Preschoolers

Reading to children has many positive effects. It supports their acquisition of language. It stimulates their play by providing new ideas. It enhances the adult-child relationship by providing an opportunity to sit together and converse. When children are read to in small groups the closeness and the shared experiences provide opportunities to develop friendships with peers. The stories children hear provide themes for their sociodramatic play. The illustrations in high-quality children's books provide visual pleasure and promote children's aesthetic development.

The quality of the books published for children varies greatly. There are a great number of excellent children's books, but there are also books of very low quality on the market. Health and Welfare Canada's (1993) booklet *Good Books for a Good Start: Choosing and Using Children's Books in Child Care* is a very helpful reference that can assist care providers in the selection of books for children. Other guides to children's literature are also available in most libraries and bookstores.

Moral Development

Few researchers have studied the moral development of preschoolers. Scholars who study the broad topic of moral development approach it from various contradictory points of view. There is no consensus among these scholars on the question of how moral development takes place. Care providers wishing to facilitate the moral development of preschoolers are provided with little guidance. Indeed, the major textbooks for care providers in training omit the topic.

Nucci and Killen (1991) reviewed recent studies of preschoolers and concluded that young children are able to distinguish between moral issues and matters of social convention. Hitting, hurting, and stealing are examples of moral transgressions. The rule to remain seated during snack time is an example of a social convention. These findings contradict the model of moral development put forward by Kohlberg (1975). Using Kohlberg's model we would expect preschoolers to be at Stage 0, which is a premoral stage, or at Stage 1 in which goodness or badness is determined by the physical consequences of an action and in which avoiding punishment and unquestioning deference to power are valued in their own right.

Although there is no research to directly support their position, Nucci and Killen advocate that care providers working with young children address moral transgressions by focusing on the effects of the acts on others. For example, hitting is wrong because it hurts others. Nucci and Killen advocate that violations of social conventions be dealt with by letting children know the reasons for the rules or expectations.

The play environment provides the context in which preschoolers' moral development occurs. The conflicts that arise between children as they play provide the moral issues. The care provider's interventions can help children learn how to resolve these issues fairly and respectfully so that the play can continue (see Box 6.3).

Box 6.3
Moral Transgressions and Social Conventions

Nucci and Killen (1991) advocate that care providers distinguish between moral transgressions and social conventions. They also advocate that responses to moral transgressions differ from responses to breaches of social conventions.

◆ A moral transgression is behavior that is objectionable on moral grounds. It is behavior that is wrong in a moral sense. Behavior that denies or prevents others from exercising their human rights is, in most cases, wrong. In the context of play, it is wrong for children to intentionally hurt one another, either physically (for example, by kicking) or emotionally (for example, by verbal insults such as name-calling).

continued

◆ A social convention does not involve moral issues. Social conventions are simply the behaviors that are preferred in a particular setting. Social conventions differ from setting to setting but standards of morality apply generally. To breach a social convention may be considered a faux pas or impolite, but it is not wrong in a moral sense. In child care settings, care providers typically establish and enforce rules of behavior that constitute social conventions. The rules facilitate smooth interactions, reduce conflicts, and allow for the safe, orderly use of the equipment and toys. For example, a care provider may establish a rule that only three children at a time may be in the sandbox. This is a social convention in this particular facility. The reason for the rule is practical. It is based on the size of the sandbox, the number of toys there, and the amount of space children need to play in the sand without disrupting one another.

Nucci and Killen suggest that care providers treat children's moral transgressions differently from their breaches of social conventions.

◆ When a child intentionally hurts another child, the behavior is described as wrong because of its effect on the other child. For example, throwing sand is wrong because sand gets into people's eyes and it hurts. It is wrong to hurt others.

◆ When a child breaches a social convention, the behavior is corrected and the child is taught the reason for the rule. For example, if there is a rule that children put the blocks back in the block basket when they are finished playing with them, the care provider explains the reason for the rule. Perhaps the rule is intended to keep the block area tidy, to prevent children from tripping on blocks, or to enable children to easily find the blocks when they want to play with them.

Nucci and Killen provide a respectful approach to guiding children's behavior. Both moral transgressions and breaches of social conventions are used as opportunities to teach children appropriate behavior. The reasons the care providers give are intended to support the children's moral development.

Play Environments for Preschoolers

Harms and Clifford (1980) identify the features of excellent environments for preschoolers. To receive the highest scores on their scale, a facility must provide ample opportunity for free play. During free play children are permitted to select materials and companions and to manage their play independently. Children can choose from a wide range of toys, games, and equipment, both indoors and outdoors. The facility contains a number of interest centers with space for play. Books, toys, games, props, equipment, and other materials are available to children. The materials support language development, reasoning, physical development, and creative expression. A highly rated play environment using the Harms and Clifford instrument includes the space, playthings, and time preschoolers need to use and refine their large- and small-muscle skills, to play alone or with others, and to actively explore and investigate.

The Harms and Clifford rating scale offers care providers guidance in creating good play environments for preschoolers. It identifies the features that "seven experts in the day care and early childhood fields" (p. 38) agreed are indicators of quality child care. It is valuable to care providers who wish to evaluate their own programs. It includes useful information that care providers can apply to raise the quality of their programs. The rating scale reflects the child development literature and prevailing standards of practice. However, the Harms and Clifford rating scale is not a template for a perfect play environment for preschoolers. There are no templates. Harms and Clifford acknowledge "the lack of universally accepted norms for early childhood environments" (p. 38).

It is futile to search for a single model of excellence. There are many ways of creating excellent play environments for preschoolers. If local appropriateness is part of one's definition of excellence, a template is not possible. Excellent programs tailor the play environment to suit the children.

Some publications for care providers include photographs and floor plans as examples of excellent play environments. The recommended environments may include elements that can be borrowed or modified or tried out in other programs in other locations. However, do not assume that the examples of excellent play environments are appropriate for all groups of children. There is no single ideal play environment that ought to be copied.

The Role of the Care Provider in the Play Environment

The care provider remains an important part of the play environment for preschoolers but less obtrusively than with younger children. Preschoolers' increasing independence, combined with their expanding social skills and enjoyment of one another, results in a new role for the care provider. The care provider becomes more and more a follower, extending or enriching the play chosen by the children, and, where appropriate, engaging them in conversations related to the play. With preschoolers, the play itself and the other children become more important and the care provider can step out of the spotlight. The care provider's role is to facilitate child-centered, child-chosen play. Enabling children to make their own play choices ensures that the play is individually appropriate and it promotes their development as decision-makers.

The care provider expects that in the course of their play the children will experience and express various emotions. The care provider accepts and labels those emotions and helps preschoolers to express them constructively. When moral issues arise, the care provider helps children distinguish between right and wrong behavior.

Using Local Materials in the Play Environment

A significant aspect of the care provider's role is the creation of the setting in which the children will play. This involves arranging the furnishings and providing equipment, toys, and other materials. The design of a play environment should be consistent with the program's goals. If the program has established as a goal the promotion of children's development in all domains, the design should support that goal. Similarly, if local appropriateness is a program goal, the design of the play environment should help to achieve that goal. The purchasing decisions made by care providers can strengthen ties with the local community. Although it is possible to equip child care facilities with high-quality manufactured products that are sold in stores and through catalogues, there are also local alternatives. For example, in many communities there are workshops employing adults with disabilities. These workshops may be able to make furnishings such as tables, chairs, easels, shelves, storage units, and outdoor equipment such as sandboxes and climbing apparatus. Woodwork classes in the neighborhood high school may be willing to make blocks or doll furniture. Local craft fairs and bazaars often sell wooden vehicles and other toys made by local hobbyists. Community groups often make and sell handmade toys, dress-up costumes, and doll clothes as fund-raisers.

Buying from these local sources will have a positive economic impact on the community along with providing opportunities to increase the local appropriateness of the child care program. For example, if you live in a fishing community, you may be able to order toy boats that resemble the boats used by local fishers. If you live in a mining community, you may be able to order toys that resemble the equipment used at the mine. Having furnishings made locally provides opportunities for interesting outings to see the workshops and meet the people who are making things for the child care facility. These people may also be invited to the facility to see how their products are being used and to meet the children.

✦ ✦ ✦ ✦ Ethical Practice

Care providers for children of all ages are continuously required to make decisions and take action in situations in which the welfare of others is at stake. Everything care providers do on the job affects others. This is an essential feature of the occupation. All of the decisions they make and all of the things they do have an impact on the welfare of others. Such decisions are by definition in the ethical domain. Care providers make these decisions on the basis of their ideas about how people ought to behave, how people ought to treat one another, and what obligations people have to one another. Everyone has a set of personal ethical principles—fundamental positions on how people ought to behave or treat one another. People do not usually articulate their personal ethical principles, but those principles underlie all of their decisions and actions. It is helpful to clarify one's personal ethical principles when entering a profession such as child care, in which practitioners are required to operate in the ethical domain. This clarity facilitates quick decision making on-the-run. It also enables care providers to explain the reasons for their decisions and practices. Parents, colleagues, and supervisors often ask care providers to justify decisions and actions. In many cases, the explanations involve references to the care provider's personal ethical principles. Being able to clearly articulate them enhances these explanations (see Box 6.4).

Box 6.4
Our Ethics Guide Our Decisions

The decisions of care providers reflect their personal and professional ethics. For example, care providers are required to decide whether preschoolers may bring to the facility their own favorite toys from home. In making this decision, care providers might consider these factors:

◆ The children who want to bring favorite toys from home will be happy if allowed to do so.

◆ Children who bring favorite toys from home will be unhappy if those toys get broken while at the facility.

◆ Other children in the facility will be attracted to the special "from home" toys that are brought in. They will want to play with them. The owners may refuse to share, citing ownership. Disputes over the toys can be expected.

◆ Children with attractive toys from home may use them to gain playmates or enhance their status in the group.

◆ Children without toys from home may resent those with toys from home.

◆ Children may pressure parents to buy toys like those brought to the facility by other children.

◆ The toys from home may represent values that conflict with those of the facility.

Ethical decision making is not a matter of selecting the option with more supporting arguments. One ethical objection to an option outweighs any number of arguments in favor of that option.

In the example above, one care provider might make the decision on the basis of self-interest, placing the ethic "Minimize personal hassles" first. He or she would not allow toys from home because disputes over toys would likely arise.

Another care provider might make the decision by giving primacy to the ethic "Support parents." He or she would not allow toys from home because they would add to the pressure on parents to buy commercial toys for their children, causing stress for parents on tight budgets.

Another care provider might make the decision by giving primacy to the ethic "Promote the well-being of the children." He or she may feel an ethical obligation to provide children with nonsexist

continued

toys that represent prosocial values. Since toys from home may represent contrary values, this care provider would decide not to allow children to bring favorite toys from home.

In this example, all three care providers made the same decision, but for different reasons. Each care provider applied his or her personal and professional ethical principles.

The professional associations that represent care providers recognize that their members are required to make decisions in the ethical domain. Many associations have developed codes of ethics that state the ethical principles that the associations agree ought to guide the on-the-job decisions of their members. Codes of ethics do not provide easy answers to the ethical issues that arise when working with children. They can, however, provide care providers with guidance. Codes of ethics outline the profession's positions on how members ought to behave, and they clarify members' professional obligations. Unfortunately, there is significant disparity in the quality of the published codes of ethics. Some are much more helpful than others. Professional ethical principles are part of the environment in which individual care providers make their decisions. Ethical practice is not simply a matter of choosing one of the better professional codes of ethics and applying it like a formula to make decisions in the ethical domain. A good code provides a valuable framework, but the analysis of the situation, the weighting of conflicting principles, and the assessment of the likely consequences of pursuing each option are usually done on-the-spot by individual care providers. Care providers' decisions, therefore, reflect their own individual points of view and their own personal beliefs, values, and ethical principles.

The Early Childhood Educators of British Columbia (1994) has developed an exemplary code of ethics. This code includes eight principles relating to all aspects of professional practice. The following principles have been selected from the eight because of their relevance to care providers planning and supporting children's play:

◆ Early childhood educators promote the health and well-being of all children.

◆ Early childhood educators use developmentally appropriate practices when working with all children.

◆ Early childhood educators demonstrate caring for all children in all aspects of their practice.

◆ Early childhood educators work in ways that enhance human dignity.

Although this code explains each principle and lists the implications for practice that follow from each principle, it cannot prescribe the right answers to the ethical issues care providers encounter. Professional ethical principles such as these are one of the considerations when care providers make decisions.

◆ ◆ ◆ ◆ Chapter 6 in a Nutshell

The following major understandings were introduced in Chapter 6:

◆ The physical development of preschoolers is characterized by the refinement of skills and increases in control and coordination.

◆ Erikson's (1950) description of preschoolers facing a crisis that he called Initiative vs. Guilt is found in many child development textbooks.

◆ Preschoolers experience and express a wide range of emotions that care providers can help them name and express in acceptable ways.

◆ Since preschoolers fail in about 70% of their attempts to establish or join play, care providers must make individual decisions about whether to teach children the more successful strategies.

◆ Parten (1932) defined six categories of social participation among preschoolers: unoccupied behavior, onlooker behavior, solitary independent play, parallel activity, associative play, and cooperative or organized supplementary play.

◆ A seventh category—empathic play—is hypothesized to follow cooperative or organized supplementary play.

◆ The development of language is one of the primary cognitive tasks for preschoolers.

◆ Care providers can help preschoolers distinguish between right and wrong behavior and between socially acceptable and socially unacceptable behavior.

◆ Excellent play environments for preschoolers should not all look alike, but they should reflect high standards of practice and suit the children and communities they serve.

◆ Care providers who work with preschoolers facilitate child-centered, child-chosen play.

◆ Furnishing the play environment provides opportunities to increase local appropriateness and develop links with community members.

◆ The decisions made by care providers involve the application of personal and professional ethical principles.

At Practicum

1. Observe a pair or threesome of four-year-olds playing associatively or cooperatively. What techniques do other four-year-olds use to try to join that play? What techniques result in acceptance? What techniques result in rejection?

2. Observe how the staff at your practicum placement respond to moral transgressions such as hitting, biting, and hair pulling. Also observe how the staff respond to violations of social conventions such as facility-specific rules of conduct. After leaving the facility, write a description of one of those incidents from the point of view of the child who committed the moral transgression or violated the social convention.

3. Spend at least one hour watching a preschooler play. Make notes of the child's activities. Afterwards, identify the domain or domains of development that were influenced by each activity.

Extend Your Learning

1. Visit the children's section of a public library. Ask the children's librarian to identify two or three books that are enjoyed by three-year-olds. Among the many benefits children derive from being read to is the acquisition of new ideas that enrich their play. How might the books recommended by the librarian enrich the play of three-year-olds?

2. Consider the impact of technological products such as electronic toys, television, video games, and computers on the play of preschoolers. Describe how these products influence each domain of a preschooler's development.

3. Interview a parent of a preschooler. Ask the parent to describe the child's strengths, interests, and favorite activities. Ask the parent what skills he or she hopes the child to develop during the next few months (short-term goals). Are the parent's goals for the child realistic for a child of this age? If you know the preschooler, are the goals realistic for this particular child? If you were that child's care provider, what play opportunities would you create for him or her? Print a "P" beside the play opportunities that will help the child reach the goals the parent has for the child.

◆ ◆ ◆ ◆ Look Inward

If you are using this book as a textbook for a course, you will not be asked to share your answers to these questions with your instructor or classmates. These questions are provided to stimulate introspection.

1. Reflect on the ethical principles that you live by. Write three or four of the principles that guide your behavior and treatment of others.

2. Obtain the code of ethics of a professional association for care providers. Do you support the principles in that code? Are there any conflicts between your personal ethical principles and the professional ethical principles endorsed by this association? If you had to decide whether or not to allow preschoolers in your care to play with toy guns, would this code of ethics assist you?

3. Can you recall incidents from your childhood in which you wanted to establish play with another child or join the play of two or more children? Do you recall your emotions when you were accepted? Do you recall your emotions when you were rejected? Do you think care providers should teach children techniques that may increase their chances of being accepted as playmates? How would you explain your position to another care provider?

Supporting the Play of School-Age Children

Objectives

◆ to explain why school-age children have insufficient play opportunities

◆ to summarize characteristics of the development of school-age children

◆ to discuss ways of involving school-age children in planning for play

◆ to suggest appropriate ways of guiding the behavior of school-age children

School-Age Children and Play

Entering Grade 1 is a major transition for children. Among the many changes in children's lives at this time are reduced opportunities for free play and new expectations on the part of adults. Although there is widespread support, particularly among the adults who work with children, for the idea that free play is appropriate, desirable, and beneficial for preschoolers, there is no comparable consensus regarding the importance of free play for children aged 6 to 12. After crossing the threshold of the Grade 1 classroom, children begin to receive from adults a different set of messages from those received during their preschool years.

At School

For most of the day, school-age children are expected to settle down, focus on their work, pay attention to lessons, follow directions, and complete their assignments during the allotted time. Teachers have curriculum guides to follow, skills to teach, and prescribed textbooks to cover. Parents and other community members expect that school-age children will gain knowledge and skills in many subjects. The serious business of schoolwork occupies most of the day. At the end of the school day, many children, particularly those in Grades 4 to 7, have homework assignments to complete. The school's primary mandate is to teach knowledge and skills—regardless of the school's philosophy, the extent to which the program is developmentally appropriate, the amount of subject integration, the prevalence of individual program planning, or the quality of the curriculum. Elementary schools are not expected to be centers for play.

After School

Children's after-school hours are spent in a variety of ways. Some children go home and are supervised by parents or other adults. When their homework is done, these children may have opportunities for free play. Because of many factors, including safety concerns, active outdoor play may not be an alternative, and the after-school hours may be spent in sedentary activities such as watching television and playing electronic games. Some children go home to what is euphemistically called "self-care" with no adult supervision. Some older school-age children are required to supervise younger siblings after school. Some families make arrangements for their school-age children to attend child care programs, take lessons such as dance or music, or participate in organized sports and athletics after school.

These structured, adult-led lessons and programs provide interesting, enriching experiences for children. They can contribute significantly to children's physical fitness, enhance their self-esteem, and introduce them to sources of lifelong enjoyment. Of the various adult-led group programs, child care programs are the only type that usually include time and encouragement for free play. Leading authors in the field of school-age child care—such as Haas-Foletta and Cogley (1990), Sisson (1990), Bender, Elder, and Flatter (1984), and Albrecht (1991)—advocate including free play in school-age child care programs. In contrast, recreation programs and sports and athletic programs generally follow the school model, with the leader or coach directing the activities of the participants.

Attitudes to the Play of School-Age Children

Compared with the preschool years, the overall pattern of the school-age years is one of less time for free play. For many school-age children, the out-of-school hours are filled with either adult responsibilities or school-like programs, resulting in limited opportunities for free play. Even children in other situations find that their opportunities for free play are limited. Many of these children have the time for free play but lack appropriate space, particularly outdoor space for large-muscle activities with friends. The difference between the play opportunities provided for most preschoolers and the play opportunities provided for most school-age children is a reflection of the beliefs and values of North American adults.

We adults are responsible for the fact that school-age children have few opportunities and little encouragement for free play. Elementary schools are places to work rather than places to play because we want children to focus on acquiring the knowledge and skills identified in elementary curricula. That is what is expected by parents and other taxpayers. Attitudes toward school-age children that became established in the days when play was viewed as just a way to run off excess energy have persisted.

Elementary school teachers are unlikely to act as play advocates or assist in the promotion of play opportunities for school-age children. In a review of college catalogues, Bowman (1990) found that play is not a significant aspect of teacher education programs. Typically, teachers in training are not introduced to the benefits children derive from play even though play enhances the attributes that are predicted to be needed to succeed in the future, such as creativity and the ability to take initiative and be self-directed.

In spite of the high costs associated with registering school-age children for recreation programs, minor sports, and various types of lessons and classes, many families prefer these school-like programs to free play. The programs have many positive features. The children are usually supervised by responsible leaders and coaches who teach the children new skills. Children often help select their programs, so they are highly motivated to attend and genuinely enjoy the activities. The drawback to an after-school schedule dominated by such programs is the cumulative effect of further reducing children's time for free play, either by themselves or with friends, or to relax (see Box 7.1).

Box 7.1
Accepting Inactivity

Good child care programs for school-age children allow the participants to choose their own activities. The children also should have the option of choosing inactivity. Although the environment may be supportive of free play and may have many attractive choices available, the children should not be required to participate in group activities or to play independently. They should have the choice of not playing, of daydreaming, or doing nothing. Albrecht and Plantz (1993) state that in developmentally appropriate school-age child care programs, care providers "respect decisions by children and youth to participate or not, even when a child or youth chooses to do nothing" (p. 7). The National Association of Elementary School Principals (1993) also identifies children's freedom to choose their activities as an indicator of excellence in school-age child care programs. The association identifies relaxation as a choice available to children in quality programs. Among the acceptable forms of relaxation is "daydreaming" (p. 18).

continued

Since children's school hours are filled with structured, compulsory activities, the after-school hours should allow children the option of choosing inactivity. Most children choose inactivity from time to time because they are tired or need time to unwind after a busy day at school. However, if a child always or frequency chooses inactivity, he or she may benefit from assistance in selecting enjoyable activities.

This overview of play opportunities for school-age children is not simply descriptive. It includes a negative assessment of the status quo, based on these assumptions:

◆ It is unhealthy for children to spend so much time sitting—at their desks in school and at home in front of their television sets or electronic games. School-age children need opportunities for active play. Their physical development is impeded by the lack of time and lack of safe, stimulating environments for play.

◆ The emotional well-being of school-age children is impaired by the absence of opportunities for free play.

◆ It is unsafe for school-age children to be at home without adult supervision.

◆ Many play environments are unsafe because of poorly designed or poorly maintained equipment or because of individuals who represent a threat to children.

◆ School-like recreation programs, lessons, sports, and athletics provide benefits to those who can afford them, but they are not a substitute for free play.

◆ Play is enjoyable. It increases children's happiness. When we allow children to play we are enhancing the quality of their lives. The developmental benefits linked with play can be achieved through other experiences, but play has the added bonus of being fun for children.

Signs of Change

Although the big picture for school-age children is one of few and shrinking opportunities for play, there are some encouraging signs. The first is the expansion of school-age child care. Some child care facilities that were originally opened for preschoolers are expanding to include before- and after-school care for school-age children. Many facilities exclusively for school-age children are being established to meet the needs of families. Few training programs specifically for school-age care providers have been available, so in many cases, staff have been recruited from graduates of early childhood care and education programs. As a result, these care providers are aware of the importance of play in children's development, and they plan programs that support all of the domains of development, as they were trained to do with younger children. Staffing school-age child care programs with early childhood specialists has had drawbacks as well. The unique training needs of school-age care providers have been identified (McDonell, 1993) and they are beginning to be met in some communities. The training programs that are being developed for school-age care providers, such as *Kids' Time* from the California Department of Education (1993) and the publications distributed by School-Age NOTES (1994), reflect sensitivity to the benefits of free play.

The second encouraging sign is the work being done by some architects and equipment designers to create safe, high-quality, developmentally appropriate play spaces for school-age children. Playgrounds have been described by Frost (1992) as "sterile, barren, hazardous places" (p. 128), "a national disgrace," and "ill-suited to the developmental needs of children" (p. 129). Although he is highly critical of most elementary school playgrounds and parks, Frost praises a number of excellent new playground designs. These well-designed play environments indicate that at least some adults have been convinced by the arguments of the advocates of play.

◆ ◆ ◆ ◆ The Development of School-Age Children

Children between the ages of 6 and 12 differ significantly in all aspects of their development. The play choices of school-age children reflect their individual developmental profiles.

Physical Development

During the school-age years children have the potential to become stronger and better coordinated. Their running speeds can increase and their endurance can improve. They can, with coaching and practice, learn complex physical skills. Good play environments provide opportunities and motivation for a variety of enjoyable physical activities to support children's physical development.

School-age children exhibit a wide range of physical differences. They range from Grade 1 children who still have all of their primary teeth to Grade 6 girls who have already entered puberty. They vary in height, weight, large- and small-muscle skills, fitness levels, and inclination toward active play. Regardless of their individual profiles, for the sake of their health, they all need to be physically active.

Children may need more than space and equipment in order to become physically active. Some school-age children require adult support and leadership. Care providers can teach them new games, teach them the skills needed to play those games, and act as coaches, providing encouragement and noticing their progress. For example, a care provider might teach a group of children one of the hopscotch games described by Simmons and Porter (1982), demonstrating how to use chalk to draw the hopscotch squares on a sidewalk, explaining the rules of the game, and providing them with buttons to use as their markers.

Concerns about Physical Development

Discussions of the physical development of school-age children must distinguish between what is and what could be. With good nutrition and exercise, school-age children have the potential to become stronger and increase their endurance and derive enjoyment from their expanding physical skills. Unfortunately, reduced opportunities for active play combined with high rates of television viewing and the growing use of video games are taking their toll. The physical development of school-age children is less than optimal. Their health is at risk because of their poor nutrition and lack of exercise. Research reviewed by Corbin and Pangrazi (1992) reveals an increase in children's body fat levels over a 20-year period. Kuntzleman and Reiff (1992) cite personal clinical observations and published research to support their conclusion that children's cardiovascular fitness levels are declining.

There is an urgent need to correct this situation. Schools ought to be providing school-age children with health education that emphasizes decision making in all of the areas that affect their health. It should also be a priority to increase the activity levels of school-age children. In a 1994 presentation to the Society for Children and Youth of British Columbia, Brian Sutton-Smith, one of the world's experts on children's play, informed the audience that children move twice as much in play as they do in physical education classes. Improved physical education classes and increased opportunities for play are both in order if we are to halt the decline in children's fitness. If communities were to provide safe, well-designed play environments, staffed by trained play leaders, they would be making a wise investment in the well-being of their most precious resource. If affordable, high-quality school-age child care programs offering opportunities for active play were available to all families, fewer school-age children would be going home to watch television, nibble on junk food, and play computer games.

Care providers who are aware of the problems regarding the physical development of school-age children ought to encourage their communities to make the changes that are needed to promote children's health.

Emotional Development

Erikson (1950) labeled the developmental crisis of the school-age years Industry vs. Inferiority. Success at this stage, according to Erikson, involves working, producing, acquiring skills, and learning to use tools. The danger at this stage is that the child will feel inadequate and inferior to "his tool partners" (p. 260) and become discouraged from pursuing a role in the society's technology and economy.

Erikson's perspective on the school-age years has been extremely influential. Elementary schools, recreation programs, minor sports organizations, children's clubs, and many individual families accept industry as a worthwhile goal for school-age children. The high value placed on work and skills and productivity is, unfortunately for the children, partly responsible for the imbalance discussed earlier. In accepting the importance of industry, our society has largely squeezed out opportunities for school-age children to play. Wishing to protect them from feelings of inferiority, we have filled their days with classes, lessons, and more opportunities to work.

Sensitivity to children's feelings of inferiority during the school-age years has produced a massive response. Institutions have sought to eliminate biases that could cause some children to feel inferior. Numerous programs have been created that attempt to compensate for the "differential opportunity" (p. 260) that Erikson noted. Remedial services have been made available to children whose skill acquisition is assessed to be atypical. Books have been written and courses have been developed that encourage adults to interact with children in ways that enhance the children's self-esteem. Regardless of the effectiveness of these initiatives when submitted to objective assessments, they have increased our awareness of the powerful long-term impact of children's feelings about themselves. For highlighting the importance of school-age children's sense of worth, we owe gratitude to Erikson.

Free play provides school-age children with opportunities for enhanced self-esteem. They select activities that match their individual stages of development. Play is something children can do their way. They use the available toys, props, and materials in ways that provide them with personal satisfaction. Open-ended playthings let children make the decisions about how they will be used. In play, the children are in the driver's seat. They can pursue their own interests and develop competence. An appropriate play environment provides all of the children with opportunities to enjoy themselves and feel good about themselves. Many play choices are available to accommodate the diversity that is a characteristic of groups of school-age children.

Social Development

During the school-age years children's peers become increasingly important to them. Their ability to make friends and maintain friendships profoundly influences their self-esteem. Although they may sometimes choose solitary play, acceptance by other children and the acquisition of interpersonal and group skills are essential to the well-being of school-age children. Children's friendships are discussed in detail in Chapter 8.

Care providers can support children's social development by teaching them effective ways of handling the interpersonal conflicts that arise during play (see Box 7.2).

Box 7.2
Conflict Resolution

Most care providers who work with school-age children have had to respond to situations in which children have used fighting as a means of handling interpersonal conflicts. After intervening to stop the fighting, many care providers use these incidents as opportunities to teach children better ways of handling conflicts. One such approach is known as no-lose conflict resolution. This approach to conflict resolution is taught in Parent Effectiveness Training (PET) and Teacher Effectiveness Training (TET) programs. The care provider guides the children through six steps:

1. The care provider helps each child clarify his or her feelings and the reasons for those feelings.

2. The care provider helps the children to generate alternative ways of expressing their feelings.

3. The care provider helps the children to identify the consequences of each of the alternatives.

4. The children choose the best alternative for their situation.

5. The care provider encourages the children to implement the alternative that they agreed was best.

6. The care provider monitors the situation. The children are asked if the alternative they chose worked for them. If not, they are helped to select and implement another alternative.

   No-lose conflict resolution has several advantages:

◆ The children's feelings are accepted.

◆ The children actively contribute to solving their own problems.

◆ An adult solution is not imposed.

◆ The children learn a useful social skill.

◆ The care provider acts as a guide and facilitator rather than a referee.

Mixed-Age Groups

One of the principles of developmentally appropriate practice in school-age child care programs developed by Project Home Safe

(Albrecht & Plantz, 1993) states that "both mixed-age grouping and same-age grouping are used to facilitate the development of peer relations and social skills" (p. 5). Project Home Safe recognizes that mixed-age groups are not always appropriate. However, when they are appropriate, Albrecht and Plantz argue that children may benefit from play in mixed-age groups. Project Home Safe has identified the following advantages of mixed-age groups:

◆ Competition may be reduced.

◆ Older children can exercise leadership.

◆ Older children can practice social skills with younger playmates who may be less threatening to them than same-age peers.

◆ Younger children learn by watching older children.

Care providers in school-age child care programs can, as research practitioners, add to the understanding of play in mixed-age groups. For example, by observing the children in their centers, care providers may be able to answer questions such as: What types of play work well with mixed-age groups? What types of play do not work well with mixed-age groups? Are the advantages identified by Project Home Safe evident among the children in this program? Do all children react the same way to mixed-age groups? What are the pros and cons of mixed-age groups?

Cognitive Development

According to Piaget, around age seven a major change occurs in the way children think. He called it the transition from the preoperational stage to the concrete operational stage of cognitive development. The transition is characterized by their understanding of conservation (see Box 7.3). Children in the concrete operational stage are able to classify objects and arrange things in a logical series. Piaget described a corresponding change in children's play at that time. He saw them moving from symbolic play to the stage of playing games with rules.

Box 7.3
Conservation

Piaget determined whether a child had entered the stage of concrete operations by testing the child's understanding of conservation. The child would be shown a ball of clay and asked to make another ball of the same size and weight. One of the balls, ball A, would be left on the table and the other, ball B, would be used to make a sausage or a pancake or would be broken up into small pieces. The child would be asked if there was still the same amount of clay in B as in ball A. The child would be asked to explain his or her answer. Children who have not yet entered the stage of concrete operations say there is more clay in the sausage than in the ball because the sausage is longer. Additional tests would be conducted to determine the child's understanding of the conservation of weight and volume. More than half of the eight-year-olds understood conservation of substance and conservation of weight. Not until age ten did more than half of the children tested understand conservation of volume (Gruber & Vonèche, 1977, p. 356).

In contrast with Piaget's observation that playing games with rules begins around age seven, the prevailing North American child care practice is to introduce simple games with rules (such as dominoes) and simple board games (such as chutes and ladders) to kindergarten children. Games such as picture lotto and other picture card games, checkers, and other board games, and sports equipment for gross-motor games are considered to be components of appropriate school-age child care environments (Harms, Jacobs & White, in press). The suitability of these games with rules for children younger than age seven is a question that care providers may wish to address. As research practitioners, care providers can observe children playing games with rules to determine the validity of manufacturers' guidelines as to age-appropriateness. Do younger children understand and follow the rules of board games or sports? Do they try to change the rules so that they can win? At what age are children able to play and enjoy games with rules?

Piaget's theory directs our attention to the change to concrete operational thinking that occurs during the school-age years. These years are also characterized by a rapidly expanding knowledge base.

School-age children are continuously acquiring new information, and learning to classify, interpret, and apply it in new situations. They are gaining the ability to analyze information and to understand relationships between ideas. They are increasingly able to combine ideas, solve problems, generate original ideas, and evaluate ideas. All of these cognitive abilities are introduced and developed in elementary curricula.

These cognitive abilities represent enormous play potential for school-age children. The cognitive skills required of the players are one of the criteria that may be used to judge the developmental appropriateness of play activities for school-age children.

The expanding cognitive abilities of school-age children ought to be reflected in the next generation of theories of play. Our perspective on the play of school-age children has been limited by the narrow focus of the cognitive-developmental theory of play on games with rules.

Moral Development

Moral development refers to the changes that take place in the way people deal with questions of right or wrong in the interpersonal realm. Researchers have found that people deal with moral issues differently. Theorists have ranked the various approaches to create hierarchies from less mature to more mature. Scholars have put forward various mechanisms to explain how the change takes place from less mature moral thinking to more mature moral thinking. As well as disagreeing about how the change occurs, scholars also disagree about the characteristics of moral maturity.

Piaget's observations and interviews with children led him to propose a system of stages of moral development (Damon, 1980). The system devised by Piaget uses the terms "moral judgment" and "morality," but, in fact, it is limited to the topic of rules. His so-called moral stages are stages in the development of children's attitudes toward rules. Piaget identified these stages:

◆ **Premoral:** No sense of obligation to obey rules.

◆ **Heteronomous:** Rules are considered permanent, sacred, and unchangeable. They are obeyed to avoid punishment.

◆ **Autonomous:** Rules are changeable. They are obeyed in the interest of interpersonal relationships.

- **Ideological:** Children can construct new rules. Children can think about rules to address political and social issues.

Kohlberg (1975) used Piaget's work as a starting point for his own research. Kohlberg developed a system of six stages of moral development extending from childhood to adulthood (see Box 7.4). According to Kohlberg's model, the most mature stage of moral development is called the universal ethical principle orientation. At this stage, people define right behavior on the basis of universal ethical principles such as justice, the equality of human rights, and respect for the dignity of individuals.

Box 7.4
Kohlberg's Stages

Kohlberg created a model of moral development that includes these stages:

Stage 1: Punishment and obedience orientation. Avoidance of punishment and unquestioning deference to power are valued in their own right.

Stage 2: Instrumental relativist orientation. Right action satisfies one's own needs. Elements of fairness and of equal sharing are present in a pragmatic "you scratch my back and I'll scratch yours" way.

Stage 3: "Good-boy—Nice-girl" orientation. Good behavior is that which pleases or helps others and is approved by them.

Stage 4: "Law and order" orientation. Right behavior consists of doing one's duty, showing respect for authority, and maintaining the social order.

Stage 5: Social-contract, legalistic orientation. Right action is defined in terms of individual rights and standards which have been critically examined and agreed upon by the whole society.

Stage 6: Universal ethical principle orientation. Right is defined by the decision of conscience in accord with self-chosen ethical principles such as justice, equality, and respect for the dignity of individuals.

continued

Kohlberg found most 10-year-olds were between Stages 1 and 2. Most 13- to 14-year-olds were between Stages 2 and 3. Most adults do not progress beyond Stage 4. Individuals at Stage 6 are extremely rare.

Kohlberg believed that movement from lower stages to higher stages takes place when people hear moral arguments that are one stage higher than their present stage. Arguments more than one stage higher cannot be understood. For example, a child at Stage 1 moves up to Stage 2 after hearing Stage 2 arguments; however, the Stage 1 child would not comprehend arguments at Stages 3 or 4.

The publication of Kohlberg's stages of moral development created what was known as the Kohlberg bandwagon. Kohlberg's model was most influential among teachers. Some teachers began using the moral decisions made by characters in literature and decisions made by historical figures as subject matter for class discussions. These discussions allowed the teachers to determine the moral stages of their students. The teachers could then introduce arguments at the next stage in order to stimulate students' moral development.

The bandwagon has now passed. Subsequent research has questioned many aspects of the theory. Among the most serious reservations concerning its validity is Gilligan's (1982) research. Gilligan found Kohlberg's stage model did not accurately describe the moral development of girls and women. Kohlberg had based his theory on research with male subjects. Gilligan's female subjects did not analyze moral problems in the same way as Kohlberg's male subjects. Gilligan's female subjects analyzed moral problems in terms of conflicting responsibilities derived from relationships. Gilligan proposed an alternative theory of moral development for women. In Gilligan's model, the most mature level is called the morality of nonviolence. At this level, moral decisions reflect concern for harmony and compassion (Travers, Elliott, & Kratochwill, 1993). Gilligan found that morally mature women have a different definition of morally right behavior than Kohlberg found. For women, behavior that results in harmonious interpersonal relationships and behavior that demonstrates compassion for others is considered morally right.

This brief overview of the topic of moral development illustrates another poor fit between the work of the scholars and the needs of front-line care providers. Once again we see a need for research practitioners to look for answers to care providers' questions. For example:

What moral issues arise when school-age children are playing? How do the children resolve these issues? Do the younger school-age children react to moral issues the same ways as older school-age children? Do the girls react the same ways as the boys? How do staff deal with moral issues that arise in the facility? Do the reactions of staff seem to be helpful to the children? Are the reactions of staff defensible? If not, what else might the staff do when moral issues arise? Answers generated by school-age care providers would be extremely valuable to the profession.

Planning Play Environments with School-Age Children

School-age children should be involved in the creation of their play environments. The care providers and children should work together on all aspects of planning the facility, from the arrangement of the furnishings, to the selection of toys, games, and equipment, to the rules of conduct. The children should participate in decisions affecting the program and the play options available to them.

During the school-age years children are able to assume more control and responsibility for planning their play and setting up their play environments. School-age children also become increasingly able to generate new play options for themselves. Older school-age children rely less on care providers to develop all of their play choices for them. They are able to come up with their own ideas for play and then approach their care providers for approval to implement their plans and for support in obtaining any necessary props or equipment.

School-age children are able to maintain interest in play themes over an extended period of time. For example, they may construct elaborate play spaces such as forts or space stations that they will want to use and expand over a long period of time. School-age child care facilities should accommodate these long-term play interests and allow the children to build structures and leave them in place for as long as they are interested in the themes. The care providers and the children should discuss and agree on the locations of such structures in order to minimize inconvenience to others using the facility.

Supporting Play in Diverse Groups

One of the realities of school-age child care programs is the great diversity among the children. The broad age span, combined with the countless individual differences in rates of development, interests, prior experiences, and personalities, present care providers with a challenge. The play experiences available in school-age programs must allow for this diversity.

In programs with large numbers of children, care providers may divide the children into two or three groups on the basis of age. Even with a narrower age range, the individual differences among the children are significant. Programs can address the challenge of diversity in these ways:

◆ Care providers can introduce games that can be enjoyed by children of different ages and skills. There are many cooperative games that are fun for individuals with differing levels of athletic or cognitive ability.

◆ Care providers can provide toys, materials, and equipment that can be used in many different ways. For example, children from the full age range found in school-age child care enjoy open-ended toys such as Lego, Tinkertoy, and construction sets. Children can build structures according to their levels of experience. Similarly, items such as large cardboard boxes, balls, outdoor climbing equipment, clay and other modeling compounds, and props for sociodramatic play are open-ended and allow for diverse play.

◆ Care providers can match each older child with a younger child as big buddies and little buddies. Occasionally, games and activities can be planned that involve the pairs of buddies playing together. For example, care providers can introduce tag games in which both the big buddy and the little buddy are "it" and both the big buddy and the little buddy have to be tagged.

◆ Many play choices can be made available. Care providers can offer a wide range of playthings and activities from which children can choose. New playthings are introduced periodically. Reference materials and newsletters such as the publications available from School-Age NOTES can help care providers to ensure their programs remain appealing to diverse groups of children. Since children may attend a facility for six years, the program must be varied so that it is enjoyable for children over that long period.

◆ ◆ ◆ ◆ Guiding the Behavior of School-Age Children

Harms, Jacobs, and White (in press) have developed an instrument for the assessment of school-age child care environments. Their vision of excellence includes opportunities for free play and the space, time, equipment, materials, and adult encouragement needed to support school-age children's development. Unlike the Harms and Clifford (1980) instrument used to evaluate early childhood environments, the school-age instrument includes an item on discipline. Discipline often presents a challenge to school-age care providers. Since many care providers who are working with school-age children do not have training specific to this age group, they often feel unsure of how to handle the discipline issues that arise.

A comprehensive discussion of child guidance is beyond the scope of this book. However, the following suggestions may be of assistance when working with school-age children:

◆   Teach children directly the behavior standards in your facility. Do not assume they know what you expect. Your standards may be different from the standards of other adults in their lives. Explain the reasons for your standards.

◆   Expect to have to reteach your behavior standards from time to time.

◆   When responding to misbehavior, do so in a way that communicates respect for the child, caring for the child, and your desire to help the child learn acceptable behavior.

◆   It is appropriate and necessary to intervene when a child's behavior infringes on the rights of others, puts anyone at clear risk of harm, or is damaging the environment.

◆   Look for explanations for misbehavior. Is it because the children do not know what is expected of them? Are they unable to foresee the danger associated with their behavior? Are they tired or bored? Are they unable to handle frustration or lacking in self-control? Are they lacking social skills? Are they copying behavior they have seen? Are they trying to get attention? Is the behavior an indication of emotional disturbance and the need for specialized services? The appropriate response to the situation will depend on the cause of the misbehavior.

- Respond in ways that enhance children's self-esteem. Look at misbehaviors as opportunities to teach children social skills rather than as situations calling for punishment.

- Model the kind of behavior you would like the children to learn.

- Strive to create a moral atmosphere that reflects your own commitment to the highest moral principles.

The behavior of the children in a child care facility profoundly affects the quality of the program, the attitudes of the children, and the work satisfaction of the staff. It is essential that children be taught to behave responsibly. A good play environment cannot exist in a facility in which anything goes. The creation and enforcement of standards of appropriate behavior are essential facets of supporting the play of school-age children.

Chapter 7 in a Nutshell

The following major understandings were introduced in Chapter 7:

- Many school-age children lack opportunities and encouragement for free play.

- Free play is available in some school-age child care programs.

- The physical fitness levels of school-age children are cause for concern.

- Erikson (1950) has been influential with his perspective on the developmental crisis of the school-age years as Industry vs. Inferiority.

- Free play provides school-age children with opportunities for enhanced self-esteem.

- Friendships with peers are important to school-age children.

- Experiences playing in both same-age groups and mixed-age groups are beneficial to school-age children.

- According to Piaget, the cognitive development of school-age children is characterized by their understanding of conservation and their ability to classify and arrange things in series, and this stage corresponds to the stage of playing games with rules.

- Kohlberg (1975) and Gilligan (1982) have proposed theories of moral development, but there are many unanswered questions regarding how care providers might promote the moral development of school-age children.

- School-age children should be involved in the planning of their play environments.

- Groups of school-age children are extremely diverse.

- Creating and enforcing standards of appropriate behavior are essential elements of caring for school-age children.

◆ ◆ ◆ ◆ At Practicum

1. Interview a school-age child in a child care program. Ask the child to identify his or her favorite aspect of the program. Ask the child to suggest something that could be done to improve the program.

2. Ask your sponsor to tell you how the facility's behavior standards were developed. Ask what the facility's policies are regarding staff responses to the misbehavior of school-age children. Later, write a summary of the information your sponsor shared with you.

3. Observe school-age children playing games with rules. Observe both indoor games such as board games and outdoor games such as soccer. Note the techniques the children use to keep the play flowing smoothly. How do they deal with the conflicts that arise?

◆ ◆ ◆ ◆ Extend Your Learning

1. Find out what after-school options are available in your community. What do the school-age children do after school and on school holidays? Give each option a "Free Play Score" from 0 to 5. A score of 0 indicates no free play. A score of 5 indicates entirely free play.

2. Visit a playground or elementary schoolyard in your community. Does Frost's (1992) description of North American playgrounds as "sterile, barren, hazardous places . . . ill-suited to the developmental needs of children" suit this play space? List three things that could be done to make it a better place for school-age children to play.

3. Select a board game that is advertised as being appropriate for school-age children. What developmental domains are involved in playing this game? List the benefits children would gain from playing this game. Identify the values and moral messages that are embedded in the game. Is it in the children's best interest to teach them those values and moral messages?

Look Inward

If you are using this book as a textbook for a course, you will not be asked to share your answers to these questions with your instructor or classmates. These questions are provided to stimulate introspection.

1. In your opinion, who should be responsible for providing children with good play environments and opportunities to play? Is it entirely a parental responsibility? What are the consequences of making this a parental responsibility? What are the arguments for and against having the community assume responsibility for providing children with good play environments and opportunities to play?

2. Recall your own school-age years. Focus on your play experiences. Do you see any connections between your play as a school-age child and the person you are today? Did you acquire through play any skills or personal qualities that have helped you as an adult? If so, what were they?

3. Reflect on Gilligan's (1982) discovery that females analyze moral problems differently than males. Do her findings match your experience? Have you noticed similar differences? What might account for the differences that Gilligan reported?

The Role of Adults in Supporting Children's Play

8

Objectives

◆ to summarize the research on the topic of adult intervention in children's play

◆ to discuss children's friendships in the context of play

◆ to identify methods that have been used to teach children social skills

◆ to discuss the need for advocacy on behalf of children's play

◆ to introduce the concept of play as a right

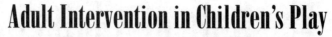

Adult Intervention in Children's Play

Most care providers would include "supporting children's play" in their job descriptions. However, there is no consensus regarding what supporting children's play should look like in practice. Among the many questions related to supporting children's play is the issue of the appropriateness of adult intervention, or involvement, in play. There is a strong tradition among care providers to avoid becoming directly involved in children's play. This issue of intervention to support or improve play is a question that every care provider needs to consider.

Smilansky's Research

An extremely influential book on adult intervention in children's socio-dramatic play was published in 1968. Sara Smilansky's *The Effects of Sociodramatic Play on Disadvantaged Preschool Children* is a classic in the research literature on the subject of play. Smilansky describes a large-scale study that she conducted in Israeli nursery and kinder-garten classes. Over 1200 children were part of her study.

This study is frequently cited for demonstrating the positive effects of having adults teach children how to engage in and sustain sociodra-matic play. This kind of intervention is called play tutoring. Smilansky found statistically significant increases in the amount of dramatic and sociodramatic play of children when teachers and experimenters "helped the children to exploit their experiences and convert their impressions into sociodramatic play material" (pp. 100–101). Even greater increases were reported in classes in which children had visits, outings, and discussions related to the themes that the adults were helping the children to exploit and convert into sociodramatic material.

Before these findings were published, adults working with young children were extremely reluctant to intervene in the children's play. Smilansky reported that in her study "all the teachers viewed any inter-vention in these activities as highly undesirable and possibly harmful to the natural development of the child's personality" (p. 142). This attitude among Israeli nursery and kindergarten teachers was prevalent among their North American counterparts at that time. The Smilansky study challenged that belief. It caused care providers to begin to recon-sider their traditional practice of noninterference in children's free play.

Over 20 years later, Smilansky (1990) summarized the positive outcomes of a number of intervention studies. The focus of these studies was children's dramatic and sociodramatic play. In all of the studies, adults intervened in a variety of ways to "improve" the children's dramatic and sociodramatic play. The interventions included:

◆ discussing possible topics for dramatic or sociodramatic play

◆ suggesting partners and interactions

◆ elaborating themes when play was underway

◆ encouraging children to adopt roles

◆ taking children on outings to provide ideas for dramatic and sociodramatic play

◆ engaging children in directed, adult-initiated fantasy

Not surprisingly, Smilansky (1990) reports that these adult interventions produced significant gains in children's dramatic and sociodramatic play activity. Smilansky concluded that dramatic and sociodramatic play provides "a strong medium for the development of cognitive and socioemotional skills" (p. 35). As a result of their participation in dramatic and sociodramatic play, children made gains in over 20 areas. For example, they developed richer vocabularies, longer attention spans, and showed reduced aggression and better emotional and social adjustment, along with many other positive outcomes. The findings summarized by Smilansky in 1990 are consistent with the results of her own earlier research (Smilansky, 1968).

Smilansky's findings have elicited interesting reactions. Smilansky (1990) reports that play tutoring has been regarded "with suspicion" (p. 40) by those who believe the ideal role for care providers is to provide a good play environment that encourages free play. Rubin and Pepler (1980) point out that Smilansky's own 1968 research data on the effects of play tutoring were nonquantitative, meaning the data were not based on measurements, and on that basis they question the significance of her findings. Smith and Syddall (1978) attribute Smilansky's 1968 research results to the tutoring rather than the play. They see the reported improvements as a function of the adult-child interactions during the tutoring. These reservations reflect the concerns of researchers with Smilansky's (1968) research design and methodology. The assumptions on which her study rests are also a source of concern (see Box 8.1).

Box 8.1
Evaluating Research Assumptions

Although Smilansky's 1968 book is best known for its contribution to the continuing discussion of whether care providers should intervene in children's play, it is also noteworthy for another reason. Smilansky's entire study rested on the belief that certain identified groups of children had deficits that resulted in their failure in elementary school. These children were all from immigrant families to Israel from various Middle Eastern and North African countries. Smilansky described these children as being "culturally deprived" compared to children whose families were from "culturally advanced countries"—meaning European countries.

Smilansky documented in detail examples of the ways in which the play behavior of the "culturally disadvantaged" children was inferior to the play of the children with European backgrounds.

Smilansky's starting point for her research is troubling. Ethical questions are raised by her assessment of cultural differences as deficits and her negative evaluation of the approaches to parenting and the behavior modeled by Asian or African immigrant families. Care providers committed to ethical practice demonstrate respect for diversity. They promote anti-bias attitudes. The underpinnings of Smilansky's research reveal a lack of respect, indeed, criticism of Middle Eastern and North African immigrant families. For example, she describes the families in these terms:

> The [culturally deprived Asian or African] child imitates *in his play the actual adult environment in which he lives. As "Mommy" or "Daddy" he gives orders, does not heed advice or answer questions . . . and if he is not obeyed, he shouts, swears, hits. (p. 30)*

> The [culturally deprived] parents . . . are simply underdeveloped within themselves, not having had the opportunity to experience life otherwise. They have not "degenerated," as might be the case with parents from privileged homes who retreat to such practices in rearing their children, but rather live their lives according to those behavior patterns and standards with which they have been confronted as children and have inherited on becoming adults. (p. 82)

Smilansky's research makes an important contribution to the play literature. It helps care providers make their decisions regarding adult intervention in children's play. However, her attitude of disapproval toward some families presents a poor example for care providers.

The Effects of Play Tutoring

Saltz and Saltz (1986) have also reviewed the research literature dealing with play training. They found that children who received highly structured play training exhibited "more frequent, more sustained, and more elaborate social pretend play during free play periods" (p. 171). In other words, the children used the skills taught during the training in their spontaneous pretend play.

Adult intervention in play is not always seen as positive in spite of the children's increase in knowledge and skills. Bowman (1990) sees play tutoring research as an example of adults using planned play activities as a means of helping children achieve learning objectives chosen by educators. Bowman acknowledges that it is possible to use play to foster knowledge and skills valued by adults. Bowman's concern is that using play in this way will reduce it to a "joyless activity" (p. 107) geared toward adult goals and lacking its "special quality" (p. 107). In other words, adult intervention in play can transform it so that it ceases to be play.

Rubin and Howe (1986) have advanced a useful definition of play:

> Play is intrinsically motivated; characterized by an attention to means rather than ends; free from externally imposed rules; laden with positive affect; and characterized by an as if, nonliteral set (pretense). (p.114)

In other words, players are motivated by the play itself; they focus on the process of the play rather than on the outcome; the players create the rules; the players feel good; and the players know the play is not real; that it involves pretending. According to this definition, adult-initiated and adult-led activities might imitate aspects of children's dramatic and sociodramatic play, but they could not be classified as play. The behaviors children demonstrate after play tutoring are probably motivated by their desire to comply with the tutor's preferences, achieve the outcomes chosen by the tutor, and follow the tutor's rules in order to gain the tutor's approval. These behaviors may resemble intrinsically motivated play, but they do not have all of the characteristics of play.

The literature on play tutoring gives a mixed view on whether adult intervention can be seen as improving children's play. In Smilansky's (1990) summary of intervention studies, the interventions varied greatly in the extent to which they intruded into the children's spontaneous play. In some cases the adults "made specific suggestions to children about what to do in order to carry out the roles more nearly completely" (p. 35). This type of extremely intrusive intervention is unlikely to produce behaviors that would fit Rubin and Howe's definition of play.

An Individual Decision

Each care provider has to decide whether or not to intervene in children's pretend play. Those who decide to intervene must decide the extent to which they will do so. This is another example of a practice issue that the research literature cannot answer for us. Each care provider's decision will reflect his or her beliefs and values and weighting of all of the factors involved.

The following analysis may assist care providers in making their decisions on this issue:

◆ The play tutoring interventions—the various suggestions, forms of encouragement, and directions—may be seen as methods of promoting children's cognitive, social, and emotional development.

◆ These interventions can be considered teaching methodologies.

◆ If, in fact, these methodologies result in the reported developmental gains, care providers may choose to use them to promote the development of the children with whom they work. The effectiveness of the methodologies in nonexperimental conditions is not assumed.

◆ The care provider may set aside his or her beliefs and values regarding children's play and focus on the question of whether or not care providers should try to directly teach knowledge and skills that they believe to be important to children's development. Some care providers believe teaching is an important part of their work, and Smilansky (1990) summarizes the benefits of play tutoring. Other care providers believe children should be allowed to discover things for themselves, a position supported by Piaget (1972), who wrote, "Every time we teach a child something, we keep him from inventing it himself" (p. 27). These two conflicting beliefs are part of the profession's heritage.

Your decision on the question of intervention in children's pretend play will reflect your beliefs regarding children's learning and development. Your explanation of your decision will rest on your beliefs and values and the results of your own experimentation and observations while working with children. You may take into account the opinions of others, but ultimately the decision is yours.

♦ ♦ ♦ ♦ Facilitating Children's Friendships

Play provides children with opportunities for social development, including the formation of friendships with other children. Friends are an important source of joy for children, and those who are unable to develop friendships are susceptible to an assortment of social and emotional problems extending into adulthood (Kupersmidt, Coie, & Dodge, 1990). The advantages of friendships with peers and the serious negative consequences of being without friends have led care providers and others who work with children to seek ways of facilitating children's friendships.

Researchers have conducted many studies involving interventions intended to help children form and maintain friendships. Much of the research has been based on the assumption that children without friends have a social skills deficit. Various experimental treatments have been used to increase children's social skills as a means of improving their acceptance by peers (Asher & Renshaw, 1981). Although many studies have been conducted, Rizzo (1989) points out that scholars do not yet understand the process by which friendships are formed and maintained.

Selman's Stages of Friendship

Selman (1981) has proposed that children's understanding of friendship changes to reflect their expanding ability to take the perspective of others. Selman described five stages of friendship:

♦ **Stage 0: Friendships based on proximity.** One's friends are one's playmates at the moment.

♦ **Stage 1: One-way assistance.** A friend does what one wants done. Friends are known better than others.

- ◆ **Stage 2: Fair-weather cooperation.** Friends coordinate their attitudes temporarily. They are unable to maintain the friendship when conflicts arise.

- ◆ **Stage 3: Intimate and mutually shared relationships.** Friendships are a source of mutual intimacy and support. Friends share their problems. Friendships survive conflicts and foul-weather incidents. Stage 3 friends are possessive of one another.

- ◆ **Stage 4: Autonomous interdependent friendships.** Friends are simultaneously independent to establish friendships with others and dependent on one another for psychological support.

A theoretical framework such as Selman's, like other stage models, is helpful to care providers in that it serves to keep our expectations realistic. When young children are unable to cooperate with one another or resolve conflicts that inevitably arise during play, they are not being naughty and the situation does not call for a disciplinary response from adults. The children may simply be at an immature stage of friendship. The appropriate response is one that is congruent with the children's level of understanding and social perspective-taking (their ability to take the perspective of others). Selman has identified the approximate ages at which children are in each stage (see Table 8.1). Although these ages are imprecise and overlapping they provide us with rough guidelines regarding the stages of friendship we are likely to observe among children.

Table 8.1
Selman's Stages of Friendship

Stages of Friendship	Approximate Ages
0: Friendships based on proximity	3 to 7
1: One-way assistance	4 to 9
2: Fair-weather cooperation	6 to 12
3: Intimate and mutually shared relationships	9 to 15
4: Autonomous independent friendships	12 to adult

A Role for Research Practitioners

Both Selman's (1981) friendship stage theory and Parten's (1932) categories of social participation outlined in Chapter 6 suggest approaches that research practitioners might explore in child care settings. Selman's model suggests that preschoolers' friendships are based on being together and knowing one another. If we provide preschoolers with opportunities to be together and become familiar with one another, friendships may develop. Parten's research and Selman's model are at odds on the question of when cooperative play may be expected. According to Selman, Stage 2, Fair-weather cooperation, is possible when children's social perspective-taking advances to the level of being able to put themselves in another's shoes and see themselves from another's point of view. Selman indicates that children develop this ability during the school-age years, roughly ages 6 to 12. However, Parten reported high frequencies of cooperative play among children aged 3 to 4.5 years (Figure 1, p. 260). In a replication of Parten's study conducted by Barnes (1971), very different results were obtained. Barnes observed the free play of three-, four-, and five-year-olds and found the children played much less socially than the children in Parten's study. Barnes's observations are more consistent with Selman's stage theory.

The available research literature indicates that play environments influence young children's interactions with their peers (Guralnick, 1986). Variables such as the type of toys and equipment available to the children, the size of the group, and the adult-child ratios all influence children's social interactions. While we are aware of some of the variables that can affect the development of friendships, the research is too sparse to guide us in the creation of play environments that are optimal for promoting friendships.

Care providers can add to the understanding of children's friendships and the environmental factors that enhance the formation of friendships by making careful observations of the children in their care.

Teaching Social Skills to Children

Children's abilities to form friendships are affected by more than just their play environments. Individual children bring to the play setting different repertoires of behaviors, different temperaments and preferences, and different levels of experience in groups. Each child has a particular set of social skills and pattern of peer interactions, which affect the child's acceptance, rejection, or neglect by peers.

Michelson and Mannarino (1986) have described the various methods researchers have used to teach children social skills. They include:

◆ **Modeling:** Children were shown live models or films of children performing the desired behaviors.

◆ **Positive reinforcement:** Children received a reward or special privilege following desired behaviors. They were ignored or removed from contact with others for inappropriate behaviors.

◆ **Coaching:** Children were instructed how to perform the desired behaviors. Children then practiced or rehearsed the behaviors and received feedback from the coach.

◆ **Problem-solving:** Children were taught how to identify interpersonal problems, generate possible solutions, and evaluate the likely consequences of choosing each alternative.

In research studies, these approaches have yielded mixed results. In some cases the children who received the experimental treatments acquired the targeted social skills, but in other cases no significant differences were found. Even when the training "worked" and the children gained the social skills, this did not automatically lead to greater peer acceptance. After reviewing the social skills research involving school-age children, Colletti-Rizzo and Calkins (1989) conclude that "the central tenet of these programs—that social skill is the arbiter in children's peer relations—appears tenuous" (p. 135). In other words, the social skill deficit explanation for why some children are without friends appears to be inadequate.

Implications for Care Providers

Textbooks and other publications for care providers in training include many statements directing adults who wish to support children's play or use play as a means of promoting children's development. However, given the small child care research base, most of the directive statements are a reflection of what Monighan-Nourot, Scales, and Van Hoorn (1987) call a "mixture of theory, myth, and personal experience" (p. 10). Although much advice is available, it is not well supported by research. The advice may be interpreted as providing insight into the authors' positions on the continuum ranging from "teach" to "let children discover for themselves."

Although there is considerable agreement regarding the goals of supporting play, facilitating peer friendships, and promoting the acquisition of social skills, there is insufficient evidence to allow us to say with confidence how best to reach those goals. There is a need for research practitioners to answer questions relating to children's social skills. For example: Are any children seeking peer interactions but being constantly rejected or neglected? What might be the reasons for each rejected or neglected child's difficulty with peers? Could changes to the play environment help those children? Could they be taught specific skills to help them gain acceptance by peers? How might such skills be taught? Did they learn the skills that were taught? Did they use the skills in play settings? Did the skills help them gain peer acceptance? Do younger children in mixed-age groups develop friendships more easily than children grouped with their peers? The answers to questions such as these, based on the experiences of care providers, would be of interest and assistance to the profession as a whole.

Advocating on Behalf of Children's Play

Although there are gaps in our understanding of children's play, there is also considerable evidence to indicate that adults are acting in children's best interests and supporting their health and well-being when we provide them with opportunities for free play. Professional care providers as a group are well aware of the benefits children derive from play. The Association for Childhood Education International (ACEI), a large international professional association, advocates that communities provide play opportunities for children (see Box 8.2).

Box 8.2
ACEI's Position on Play

Established in 1892, the Association for Childhood Education International is a nonprofit organization for professionals involved in the education of children from infancy through early adolescence. One of its purposes is to "focus the attention of the public on the educational needs and inherent rights of children and programs for their well-being—in their school, community and home." ACEI advocacy work has included the publication of a position paper on play entitled *Play: A Necessity for All Children* (Isenberg & Quisenberry, 1988).

In this position paper ACEI "recognizes the need for children of all ages to play and affirms the essential role of play in children's healthy development" (p. 138). ACEI advocates that communities adopt the following principles in order to assure the healthy development of all children:

◆ "We must provide appropriate play activities and equipment." (p. 142)

◆ "We must provide safe and inviting environments." (p. 142)

◆ "We must provide appropriate, planned outdoor play environments." (p. 143)

◆ "We must provide for carefully planned curricula." (p. 143)

◆ "We must assume responsible parent/teacher roles." (p. 144)

Among the many hats worn by care providers is the advocate's hat. Care providers often act as advocates on behalf of children, educating the public on matters related to the well-being of children. Given the generally sorry state of services and facilities for children throughout North America, this advocacy work is certainly necessary. One facet of the advocacy work is to make adults in the community more aware of the importance of children's play. Before communities can be expected to take action such as providing good quality care and education programs for children, they need information. Most adults are simply not aware of the value of providing children with good play environments.

Care providers face the challenge of convincing other adults in the community that children's play ought to be supported at the community level. The children can't speak for themselves. If care providers don't speak up on behalf of the children, conditions are unlikely to improve. Through casual conversations and formal presentations, care providers can make the case for community support for children's play. In your own community, you can make others aware of both the benefits children derive from play and the benefits communities derive from nurturing happy, healthy, secure, confident children who feel good about themselves. The quality of life in the community is inextricably linked to the community's collective treatment of its children.

In advocating for improved services for children, care providers can expect to be opposed by some community members. Some individuals may argue that services for children are not their responsibility and that the parents should see that the needs of their children are being met. This argument reflects support for a vision of a community consisting of independent, self-sufficient households in which each family looks after its own members. This vision is faulty in two significant respects. First, it is an inaccurate representation of community life. Each household is not independent. Everyone is affected for better or for worse by the way in which children are cared for and educated. Everyone has an interest in seeing that all children in the community receive the best care and education possible. When children receive poor quality care, everyone ultimately suffers the consequences. Second, a fragmented, disconnected community of separate, isolated households would not be a pleasant environment in which to live. It is our interpersonal relationships with others, the friendships and bonds we create with others, that determine our quality of life. A community in which the prevailing ideology is "Look out for number one" is an impoverished community without enduring sources of satisfaction or peace of mind for its citizens.

Play as a Right

In November 1989, the United Nations General Assembly adopted the *Convention on the Rights of the Child.* Article 31(1) of the Convention includes play as one of children's rights:

> States Parties recognize the right of the child to rest and leisure, to engage in play and recreational activities appropriate to the age of the child and to participate freely in cultural life and the arts.

Recognizing children's play as a right has significant implications for the countries that have signed the Convention and for all of the adults who care for children. By acknowledging that children have a right to play, adults are accepting responsibility for ensuring that children are able to exercise that right. The inclusion of play in the *Convention on the Rights of the Child* provides advocates of play with a pre-eminent source of support for the position that we ought to be providing all children with opportunities to play. The Convention is an eloquent statement that can show the way for countries and communities that are committed to making their children's well-being a priority.

The acceptance of play as a right requires governments to put in place the necessary infrastructure and provide support for children's play. Although the Convention was adopted by consensus in the General Assembly, there is still much work to be done before the vision of the Convention becomes a global reality. Care providers can advance this vision by telling community members about the Convention and by urging their elected representatives to ratify the Convention and to pass legislation that is consistent with the Convention's principles.

◆ ◆ ◆ ◆ Chapter 8 in a Nutshell

The following major understandings were introduced in Chapter 8:

◆ Research by Smilansky (1968) reported many positive outcomes when adults taught children how to engage in sociodramatic play.

◆ Other researchers have concerns about adult intervention in children's play.

◆ Care providers' decisions on the question of intervention in children's pretend play reflect their individual beliefs and values.

◆ Play provides children with opportunities to form friendships with other children.

◆ Selman (1980) has described five stages of friendship that reflect children's ability to take the perspective of others.

◆ Care providers can, as research practitioners, add to our incomplete knowledge of how to facilitate peer friendships.

- Care providers act as advocates on behalf of children.

- Community support for children's play is a means of improving the quality of life for all community members.

- The United Nations' *Convention on the Rights of the Child* includes play as one of children's rights and it can be used to bolster the position of advocates of play.

◆ ◆ ◆ ◆ At Practicum

1. Ask your sponsor to identify two children he or she considers to be friends. Observe those children while they are playing. In which of Selman's stages of friendship do these children appear to be? What behaviors led you to classify them as being in that stage?

2. Look at your practicum placement from the point of view of friendship promotion. List all of the features of the environment that make it a good place for children to make friends. For example, describe features such as the use of space, arrangement of furnishings, available equipment and toys, and the tone of the facility that support positive peer relationships.

3. Identify a child who is popular with other children in the group. Observe that popular child during free play. Look for reasons for the child's popularity with his or her peers. What social skills does the child use? What personal attributes appear to attract others? Write a one-page report summarizing your analysis of this child's popularity.

Extend Your Learning

1. Children learn social skills from the models they see. Select a television program that is popular with children. Watch one episode of that program. Focus on the interpersonal behaviors of the characters in the program. Evaluate these characters as models for young children. If children copy the behaviors of these models, will they be more or less likely to be able to establish friendships and gain acceptance by peers?

2. In Barnes's (1971) replication of Parten's (1932) study, he found significantly less cooperative play. Barnes wondered if the toys available to children in the 1970s were responsible for the differences in children's play. He considered the possibility that the toys available to his subjects were more conducive to solitary play than the less elaborate toys used by Parten's subjects during the 1920s. Consider the toys available to children today. Look at a catalogue or sale flyer distributed by a toy retailer. Randomly select 10 toys for preschoolers. Classify the toys in terms of the play they are likely to elicit. Which toys are more conducive to solitary play? Which toys are more conducive to social play?

3. Discuss with a friend who is not a child care professional the issue of the community's interest in children's play. Listen to your friend's views. Ask questions to clarify your understanding of your friend's opinions. The goal is to learn what your friend thinks about this issue, not to debate or try to change his or her opinions. Summarize your friend's views in a brief report. Protect your friend's privacy by using a fictitious name in your report. At the end of your report estimate the percentage of overlap between your own views and your friend's views on this issue. For example, 0% means you completely disagree on this issue and 100% means you completely agree with your friend on this issue.

✦ ✦ ✦ ✦ Look Inward

If you are using this book as a textbook for a course, you will not be asked to share your answers to these questions with your instructor or classmates. These questions are provided to stimulate introspection.

1. Where do you place yourself on the continuum ranging from "teach" to "let children discover for themselves"? What reasons would you give to support your position?

2. Evaluate your own friendships using Selman's Stage 4 as the standard. Do you receive from your friends the psychological support you need? Do you provide your friends with the psychological support they need? What could you do to enhance your own friendships?

3. Consider your own readiness to encourage members of your community to make changes that will enable children to exercise their right to play. Which of these ways of advocating for children's right to play do you feel comfortable with today?

   ◆ Discussing play with a friend or relative

   ◆ Discussing play with a small group of friends or relatives

   ◆ Making a speech to a group of people you know well

   ◆ Making a speech to a group of people you do not know

   ◆ Writing a letter to the editor of the local newspaper

   ◆ Phoning a radio open-line program

   ◆ Writing a letter to an elected official such as a member of the parks board or a member of the school board

   ◆ Meeting with an elected official

   ◆ Organizing a petition

   ◆ Putting up public information posters in your neighborhood

   ◆ Wearing a T-shirt with a printed message about play

   ◆ Organizing a public event to draw attention to children's right to play

9

Troubling Aspects of Play

◆ ◆ ◆ ◆ Objectives

◆ to identify appropriate responses to play that hurts others

◆ to identify appropriate responses to play that involves sexual curiosity

◆ to guide care providers who suspect a child is being abused

When Play Hurts Others

The North American view of play is overwhelmingly positive and upbeat. As a society, we associate play with happiness, fun and games, laughter, friends, and joy. The child models in the toy catalogues are smiling or laughing. Happy children's faces illustrate the boxes in which toys are packaged. When we visualize children playing, we imagine happy scenes of children enjoying themselves.

Certainly an objective observer of children's play will see happy faces and other indicators of enjoyment. One of our motives as care providers is to provide children with opportunities to experience the joyous aspects of play. The objective observer of children's play will also see that it is not all fun and laughter. Play is sometimes unpleasant. Children sometimes hit, kick, bite, insult, tease, exclude, torment, and otherwise hurt one another. They can be destructive, nasty, and cruel. This hurtful side of play comes with the territory. Just as the images of babies used in ads for disposable diapers and baby food fundamentally misrepresent the task of caring for an infant by omitting the difficulties that are part of the job, the popular images of children's play omit a significant aspect of play. Professional care providers encounter both sides of play and need to be prepared for the unpleasant as well as for the enjoyable aspects.

The Care Provider's Response

Incidents of hurtful behavior can be minimized by constant supervision of children's play but they cannot be completely avoided. Care providers' responses to hurtful incidents that occur during play reflect their beliefs, values, ethics, and approaches to child guidance. Before assuming responsibility for the care and education of children, care providers should think about how they will respond and their reasons for choosing those responses. This planning gives them carefully considered tools to use when needed. Without a planned response, in the heat of the moment—for example, when a child is hitting a playmate and the victim is screaming and crying—care providers may react unprofessionally. In the stress of the moment care providers may copy the responses of their own care providers or other adults with poor child guidance skills.

You may find the following considerations and suggestions useful during your planning:

◆ It is appropriate and necessary to intervene and stop a child who is physically or emotionally hurting or otherwise infringing on the rights of other children.

◆ Children should be taught directly that both physical and emotional hurting are wrong and are not permitted.

◆ Children should be encouraged to assert themselves to let one another know when they are being hurt or bothered. They can be coached to tell their playmates to stop. The care provider should intervene if a child's call for an end to some hurtful or bothersome behavior does not end it.

When a child is hurt by another child during play, the incident should be noted in your daily records and in the files of the children involved and the parents of both children should be informed. The documentation of the incidents may be helpful in justifying the provision of specialized services for children who frequently hurt others. Parents have a reasonable expectation that their children will be kept safe from harm while they are in child care facilities. Parents should be told what happened and how the incident was handled by the staff. When you inform parents that their children were involved in hurtful incidents, these conversations should be private, away from the children and other parents. Whether their children were either hurting others or being hurt, you should describe the incidents to parents fully and honestly without naming the other children. Parents may later learn the names of the children involved by questioning their own children, but, to protect the privacy of the other children involved, that information should not be offered by the care provider.

When Play Involves Sexual Curiosity

Children's play themes may include sexual references that can be disconcerting to care providers. Most of the sex play of young children is an expression of normal curiosity about their bodies and the differences between boys and girls. Care providers can expect to observe preschoolers playing in ways that can be classified as sexual exploration. Johnson (1993) states that sex play among preschoolers is natural and to be expected. Johnson explains:

> Preschoolers are trying to find out about the world, how it smells, tastes, works, sounds and feels. Everything related to the genitals, breasts, differences between males and females, and procreation are subjects of preschoolers' exploration and curiosity.

Romance themes in preschoolers' sociodramatic play are usually a reflection of their observations of teenagers or adults in their lives or the television programs they have seen. Providing the play does not involve exploitation, neither type of play calls for the immediate cease-and-desist response that we use with hurtful behavior. Preschoolers' play behaviors that indicate mutual curiosity and exploration do not call for a disciplinary response. Sex play that indicates curiosity is not a moral transgression. The most appropriate adult response is to treat it in a matter-of-fact way. For example, if two preschoolers have removed their underwear and are showing one another their genitals (a behavior to be expected) the care provider may calmly describe the behavior, saying, "You are noticing how your bodies are made." Remaining clothed may be treated as a matter of social convention. For example, the care provider might explain that clothes are left on because they keep us warm and they protect us from scratches and slivers. Our underwear prevents germs from spreading from us to the things we sit on and from the things we sit on to us, and underwear covers private parts of our bodies.

While preschoolers commonly reveal their sexual curiosity in their play, school-age children are more likely to do so "outside of the awareness of adults" (Krivacska, 1990, p. 88). Krivacska attributes this secrecy to the fact that older children know that adults "frown upon or actively disapprove of childhood expressions of sexuality" (p. 88).

The Care Provider's Response

The care provider's response to play that reveals sexual curiosity will depend on several considerations:

◆ The ages of the children: Playing involving mutual looking and touching by preschoolers is to be expected. Among school-age children, such play may be a cause for concern.

◆ Assessment of the extent to which the behavior is voluntary: Exploratory play between peers of comparable developmental levels is of little concern. Similar behavior involving children of different ages or levels of maturity is a cause for concern. The younger, less mature child may have been coerced or manipulated by the other child.

◆ Frequency of sex play: Occasional exploratory sex play is to be expected. A care provider should be concerned about a child who frequently or repeatedly becomes involved in exploratory sex play.

◆ Nature of the sex play: Typical exploratory sex play does not cause pain or injury. Intrusive behaviors such as putting objects into the genitals of another child and other hurtful explorations are cause for concern.

If a child is being or is about to be hurt or exploited by another child's inappropriate sex play, the care provider should intervene and redirect the play. Children who engage in age-inappropriate, coercive, or intrusive sex play, and the children for whom sexual exploration is a frequent play theme, may require professional services. Care providers who work with children who exhibit these atypical behaviors should consider consulting a qualified specialist in child development. Atypical sex play may be an indicator of abuse.

Constant supervision of children's play will minimize incidents of inappropriate sex play. Opportunities for intrusive and coercive sex play can be reduced by arranging furnishings in such a way that there are no play spaces that are out of the care provider's sight. When children have been involved in exploratory sex play, either typical or atypical, it should be documented and the parents should be told what happened and how the staff responded. As with incidents of hurtful play, this information should be communicated in private and the other child or children involved should not be named.

When Play Suggests Abuse

Although most children's behaviors classified as sex play are not indicators of abuse, there are some exceptions. Play that reveals uncommon knowledge of adult sexual behavior—beyond romance themes such as boyfriend-girlfriend role playing—may be an indicator that the child has seen the behavior or has seen adult movies representing that behavior. It could also indicate that the child has been sexually abused. The care provider's assessment of the situation is of great importance. Young children's knowledge of adult sexual behavior should be a red flag for care providers and it should not be ignored. Children who are very withdrawn and reluctant to play, as well as children whose dramatic or sociodramatic play represents verbally abusive adults, may have been emotionally abused.

The discussion here has focused on indicators of maltreatment that may appear in children's play. There are many other physical and behavioral indicators of abuse. Care providers should become familiar with the signs of abuse unrelated to play. Comprehensive lists of these signs can be found in Layman (1990) and other reference materials on child abuse.

The Care Provider's Response

A care provider's immediate response when a child's play reveals age-inappropriate knowledge of adult sexual behavior or themes of adult violence toward children will depend on whether the child is playing alone or with another child or children. In situations involving other children, the care provider should intervene and redirect the play so as to protect the other children from harm or from a potentially frightening or upsetting experience. If the child is playing alone, for example, with dolls, it is not necessary to intervene and redirect the play.

Care providers should avoid quizzing the children or otherwise acting as investigators. The interviewing of children in abuse cases is a specialized skill best left to trained, experienced social service workers. Indeed, there is a possibility that a well-intentioned care provider could, by inappropriate questioning, make it more difficult for investigators to determine whether or not abuse has actually occurred.

If you suspect a child is being or has been abused, in many jurisdictions you are legally required to report your suspicion to the social service agency responsible for child protection. Abuse may include sexual, physical, or emotional abuse. The standard for reporting suspected abuse is not proof or certainty. Child protection workers investigate the reports they receive to determine whether or not children are in need of protection. If you live in a jurisdiction that does not legally require you to report suspected cases of child abuse, it is in the children's interest that you report your suspicions.

Assisting Abused Children

Child care settings can be beneficial to children who have been abused. Through play they may express feelings they are unable to put into words. Children's relationships with their care providers may be islands of stability during periods of turbulence. Older children may want to talk to their care providers about their experiences or about the changes in their lives if their home situations have changed after abuse was revealed. Although care providers are not counselors or therapists, their caring relationships with children can be of help, especially when care providers listen and communicate acceptance. Abused children need to know that they did nothing wrong and that the abuse was not their fault. Since they are responsible for groups of children, care providers are usually unable to provide the amount of one-to-one time an abused child needs. They can, however, help children get the counseling support they may need from the appropriate community agencies.

Care Providers and the Troubling Side of Play

The discussion of the unpleasant aspects of play—play that is hurtful; sex play that is age-inappropriate, coercive, or intrusive; and play that suggests abuse—has dealt with the topics in an intellectual way. The behaviors were described and appropriate responses were outlined. It might appear that this topic is just like any other topic related to children's play. In fact, the troubling side of play is different from most other topics introduced throughout this book because of its ability to elicit strong emotional responses in care providers.

Preparing for a career as a care provider is an emotional experience. Studying topics such as child development and learning appropriate child care methods usually cause students to recall their own childhood experiences. This is sometimes painful. Students whose childhood experiences were difficult often relive unpleasant feelings that were left behind long ago.

Reading about the unpleasant aspects of play is more than an intellectual exercise. It can trigger strong emotions. If we caused hurt, saw others hurt, or were ourselves hurt, the incidents may come back to us. Our own experiences of sex play are recalled. If we coerced our playmates or were ourselves coerced, we may recall the experiences. The reactions of our care providers to our childhood sex play, whether typical or atypical, are often vivid memories. Just reading the word "abuse" is enough to cause some people discomfort. Students who saw or personally experienced abusive adults may find addressing the topic very painful. Those who have no personal knowledge of abuse may find it upsetting to confront the fact that many children are abused.

Emotional responses to these topics are normal and predictable. Strong emotions can be confusing and put us off balance. If reading and thinking about the troubling side of play has caused you to relive painful events, you may want to share your feelings with a trusted friend or with a counselor. Both friends and counselors can be very helpful in supporting and assisting people who are recalling troubling memories and emotions.

◆ ◆ ◆ ◆ Chapter 9 in a Nutshell

The following major understandings were introduced in Chapter 9:

◆ Care providers should plan in advance how they will respond to hurtful incidents that occur during play.

◆ Children should be stopped from hurting other children or otherwise infringing on the rights of other children.

◆ Parents should be told when their children hurt or are hurt by other children and also how staff handled these incidents.

◆ Preschoolers' play that reflects sexual curiosity can be expected and is not a moral transgression.

◆ The care provider's response to play that reveals sexual curiosity will depend on the ages of the children, whether the play is voluntary, and the frequency and nature of the play.

◆ Atypical sex play may be an indicator of abuse.

◆ Parents should be informed when their children have been involved in typical or atypical exploratory sex play.

◆ Care providers should not try to investigate suspected abuse but should report their suspicions to the responsible social service agency.

◆ Studying the troubling side of play can be upsetting and painful and some readers and care providers may need support from friends or a counselor.

At Practicum

1. Cases of abuse in child care facilities, although rare, have been widely publicized. What safeguards are in place at your practicum placement to protect children from abuse by strangers, by visitors to the facility, or by staff?

2. While you were at your practicum placement this term, did you see any examples of the hurtful side of play? If so, recall one incident that you observed but did not handle—an incident that was handled by your sponsor or another staff member. Write a brief description of the hurtful behavior. What, if any, was your emotional response to the hurtful behavior? What, if any, was your emotional response to the way in which the staff handled the incident?

3. Imagine that a new preschooler is going to be joining the group at your practicum placement. The child's foster mother has informed the director that the child was physically and emotionally abused as an infant and toddler. List all of the features of the play environment in your practicum placement that make it a good place for this child.

Extend Your Learning

1. Go to your public library or college library and locate some books on the topic of child abuse. Use those books to make a list of warning signs that may indicate a child is being or has been abused sexually, physically, or emotionally. Make two photocopies of your list. Exchange lists with two of your classmates.

2. Make inquiries to find out what assessment services are available in your community for children exhibiting atypical hurtful play. How do care providers access those services for the children in their care?

3. Find out how to report suspected child abuse in your community. What agency is responsible for investigating reports of suspected abuse? Contact that agency to learn the legal obligations of citizens in your jurisdiction when they suspect a child is being or has been abused. Find out how reports of suspected abuse are acted upon.

◆ ◆ ◆ ◆ Look Inward

If you are using this book as a textbook for a course, you will not be asked to share your answers to these questions with your instructor or classmates. These questions are provided to stimulate introspection.

1. Recall your own childhood. Can you remember seeing examples of the unpleasant side of play? If you can, focus on one incident. Describe the behavior of the children involved. Describe the response, if any, of the adults who were present. Knowing what you know now, was the adult response appropriate? If, as a care provider, you see children involved in a similar incident, how will you respond?

2. Preparing to respond appropriately to children's play that indicates curiosity about their bodies may bring to mind attitudes our parents and care providers taught us. What messages did your parents and care providers give you regarding your body? Did those messages help you to learn a positive attitude toward your body?

3. Make a list of the first 10 words and phrases that come to mind when you hear the words "child abuse."

Selecting Playthings

Objectives

◆ to propose that equipping a play environment reveals a care provider's knowledge, beliefs, and values

◆ to introduce factors to be considered when selecting playthings

Play Environments Reveal Their Creators' Values

Good play environments are equipped with developmentally appropriate and locally appropriate toys, apparatus, props, materials, and miscellaneous objects that children are encouraged to explore and use. The playthings that are available to children influence the play that takes place in each play environment. A significant aspect of the care provider's job is the provision of suitable playthings.

The selection of playthings requires care providers to integrate all of their professional knowledge. Equipping play environments for children involves applying an understanding of the various domains of child development, sensitivity to safety issues, awareness of the importance of play, knowledge of the local community, clear program-planning goals, and ethical decision-making skills. While the care providers' relationships with children reveal their personalities, the playthings and physical environments they provide for children reveal what they know, believe, and value. The task of equipping a child care facility requires care providers to synthesize the many strands of their professional education, including self-awareness. The playthings selected demonstrate unambiguously the care providers' interpretation of the concept of quality care and their priorities for the children in their care. Play environments show visitors where care providers stand on many child care issues. Unlike the written philosophy statements found in policy manuals, the play environments care providers create always accurately communicate their visions of child care.

The selection of toys and other playthings is a challenging exercise in decision making, taking into account many important considerations.

Safety

The playthings provided for children must not expose them to unreasonable risk. No environment is perfectly risk-free. The care provider's responsibility is to minimize risks using the standard of reasonableness. Reasonableness must be decided by the care provider on an item-by-item basis, taking into account the individual characteristics and prior experiences of the children who will have access to the playthings.

An essential part of the care provider's job is to teach children how to use playthings safely, so as to prevent injuries. Playthings should not be rejected as inherently unsafe if, with adult guidance as to their safe use, they could pass the reasonableness test. Similarly, items that appear to be safe for the intended users may require adult guidance to prevent them from being used in an unsafe manner. For example, care providers need to teach young children that tricycles may not be driven into people or into other tricycles.

Developmental Considerations

Playthings should be developmentally appropriate for the intended users. Care providers combine their knowledge of the development of typical children with their knowledge of the unique characteristics of the individual children in their care in order to select appropriate playthings. A balanced play environment includes playthings that encourage children's development in all domains.

Local Considerations

Playthings can help children become familiar with the local community. Items related to local community life are an important part of a locally appropriate play environment. The playthings should include locally made and locally gathered objects as well as objects that reflect the traditions and activities of people in the community (see Box 10.1).

Box 10.1
An Illustration of Local Differences

In most North American communities, particularly in urban centers, people associate guns with crime and violence. Care providers in those communities typically do not equip child care facilities with toy guns. In those communities guns represent anti-social attitudes and behaviors. Toy guns are considered to be inappropriate and inconsistent with the goal of promoting prosocial attitudes and behaviors.

continued

However, in some North American communities, people do not have this negative attitude toward guns. For example, in First Nations communities in northern Canada, guns are associated with hunting. Hunting is a highly respected skill. Families depend on hunters to supply a significant amount of their food. Guns are seen as essential for survival. Hunting enables families to enjoy traditional foods, which are preferable to processed commercial foods. In these communities guns do not represent anti-social attitudes or behaviors. Parents and care providers in these communities may consider toy guns and other hunting equipment to be appropriate playthings, and children's sociodramatic play may be based on their observation of hunters.

Environmental Considerations

When selecting playthings, care providers should consider their environmental impact on the planet. They might evaluate both the toys and the packaging, considering whether the packaging can be recycled in the community or whether it will end up as garbage, and whether the plaything is sturdy enough to stand up to heavy use over a long period of time or whether it will probably break and become garbage. Further considerations include the energy needed to transport the item from the factory to the care provider's community and the manufacturer's reputation on environmental issues.

The care provider's individual purchasing decisions may seem at first glance to be insignificant in the face of global environmental problems. Each person can, however, contribute to solving those problems if the environmental impact of individual choices is considered. The "green" plaything will probably be made closer to your home, built to last, packaged in a recyclable material, and manufactured by a company with a good environmental record.

Ethical Considerations

When care providers select toys and other playthings for children to use, they are operating in the ethical domain. Their decisions have far-reaching consequences. The purchase of playthings involves doing business directly with retailers and indirectly with toy manufacturers. Giving business to one retailer rather than another and purchasing a product made by one manufacturer rather than another are more than just economic decisions. They are also opportunities for individuals to make choices on the basis of ethical principles, for example by supporting companies that demonstrate a commitment to values that fit with their own.

There are research organizations such as EthicScan Canada and the Council on Economic Priorities as well as individual business journalists who monitor and report on the ethical performance of large companies. Before making purchasing decisions, care providers might choose to research and take into account the ethical profiles of the manufacturers or retailers with whom they are considering doing business. Care providers may wish to consider factors such as these:

◆ Does this company treat its employees respectfully and fairly?

◆ What is this company's record on issues affecting the well-being of children, such as child care services for employees and parental leave?

◆ Is the company a good corporate citizen, supportive of the community in which it operates?

◆ What is the company's ethical track record? Does it have a record of honesty and a commitment to integrity in all aspects of the business?

◆ If the company advertises on television, what type of programs does it sponsor? Are those programs a positive influence on children and other viewers?

Finding answers to questions such as these in a library or on a computer network requires a lot of time. An interested parent or board member might be asked to assist with researching the ethical profile of a toy manufacturer or retailer. The findings can be shared with other care providers in the newsletters published by local professional associations.

The combined value of the purchases by child care facilities throughout North America represents a significant amount of money. When manufacturers and retailers of playthings see that corporate ethics are important to care providers, companies may become more sensitive to ethical issues and those with poor ethical profiles may change some of their practices.

Social Impact

Playthings can either encourage or discourage prosocial behavior. Consider the type of play that a plaything is likely to elicit. Although fewer toy weapons are being offered for sale in toy stores, there are many heavily advertised armed action figures representing characters from television programs. These weapon-laden figures typically elicit anti-social play such as attacking and shooting others—actions that mimic the behaviors of the characters in the television programs. Toys of this type are inappropriate because they are incongruent with our professional commitment to foster children's social development, which includes acquiring prosocial attitudes and skills.

In spite of small steps toward gender equality in some areas of North American society, many toys communicate messages that counteract these steps forward. If care providers look at the catalogues distributed by major toy retailers or visit toy stores or toy departments, they see that the toy industry has different expectations for girls than for boys. The toys perpetuate stereotypes that do a disservice to both sexes. In selecting playthings for children, care providers should consider the sex-role messages the playthings convey and avoid toys that by their packaging or in their advertising communicate that they are just for boys or just for girls.

Imagination and Creativity

The playthings available to children may either stimulate or stifle creative, imaginative play. For example, a battery-operated or wind-up toy that performs some action may be momentarily amusing, but the action is all in the toy. The child is just a spectator. A plain toy, without the battery or wind-up feature, requires the child to do more than just watch, and it is a better choice as a means of encouraging imaginative or creative play.

Children's Interests

Playthings should reflect the interests of the children in the program. By listening to children, care providers can learn what topics interest them. Those interests should be kept in mind when purchasing new playthings.

Play Value

Children play because it is fun. It is one of their sources of joy and one of their ways of pursuing happiness. The playthings provided for children should be selected with fun in mind—their ability to bring about the "positive affect" that is part of Rubin and Howe's (1986) definition of play that was quoted in Chapter 8. "Play value" refers to the enduring attractiveness of playthings—the extent to which children will play with them over time. Toys with high play value can be contrasted with novelty items that are temporarily enjoyable, but do not elicit sustained use.

There are excellent reference materials available to assist care providers and others who are interested in researching the play value of commercial toys. For example, the *Toy Buying Guide* (Braiman-Lipson et al., 1988) and the annual publication *The Toy Report* (Levine, 1995) contain parents' ratings of toys based on how their children used them in home settings. The children's magazine *Zillions: Consumer Reports for Kids* includes children's ratings for various products, including games and playthings.

◆ ◆ ◆ ◆ Finding Appropriate Playthings

After taking into account all of these considerations, care providers might reasonably conclude that many of the toys for sale in local stores are unsuitable for the children in their care. This is unfortunately the case. Frost (1992) says bluntly, "The vast majority of toys purchased for children are of little or no value" (p. 70). One might add to that condemnation the observation that many are also objectionable because of their negative environmental or social impact.

Although professional care providers are likely to reject, for various reasons, many of the toys on the market, there are, nevertheless, many excellent playthings available. The toys available in toy stores are not all inappropriate; the key is to be selective. In addition, playthings need not be items marketed as toys. For example, empty boxes, household utensils, lumberyard scraps, empty plastic containers, sand, water, natural items such as leaves and pine cones and pebbles collected on outings, dress-up clothes, and odds and ends from garage sales and swap meets—all these have play value.

Research practitioners could make a valuable contribution to the field by observing children's use of playthings and documenting answers to questions such as: What playthings are most often chosen by children in each age group? What play themes are elicited by those playthings? Which playthings elicit cooperative play? Which playthings elicit aggressive, anti-social play? Which playthings elicit the most varied, creative play? Which playthings elicit the least varied play? By sharing their answers to such questions, care providers could help one another in the selection of appropriate playthings.

Chapter 10 in a Nutshell

The following major understandings were introduced in Chapter 10:

◆ The selection of playthings requires care providers to synthesize and apply all of their professional knowledge.

◆ The play environments that care providers create reveal their knowledge, beliefs, values, and positions on child care issues.

◆ When selecting playthings, care providers must consider factors such as safety, developmental appropriateness for the intended users, local appropriateness, environmental impact, the ethical profiles of the manufacturers and retailers, the social impact, the effect on children's imagination and creativity, the children's interests, and play value.

◆ Although many of the toys on the market do not meet care providers' criteria, items other than toys have play value.

At Practicum

1. List five of the playthings in your practicum placement. Beside each one note the adult values that are revealed by having that item in the play environment.

2. Take to your practicum placement a plaything that will help the children become familiar with any aspect of the local community. If necessary, teach the children how to use it safely. Observe children using the plaything. Describe the play it elicits.

3. Actively observe children's use of two or three of the most popular playthings in your practicum placement. Evaluate the social impact of those playthings. Do they encourage or discourage prosocial behavior?

Extend Your Learning

1. Consult a consumer's guide to commercial toys such as *Toy Buying Guide* or *The Toy Report*. Identify one toy for preschoolers that the guide rates highly for its play value. How would you rate that toy for its local appropriateness, environmental impact, and social impact?

2. Research the toy safety laws that are in place in your jurisdiction. Contact the government department responsible for administering toy safety laws and find out how citizens can initiate an investigation if they believe a toy is unsafe.

3. Watch some television programs that are popular with children. Watch for commercials for toys. Select any two toy commercials. Briefly describe the toys and the commercials. Make a checklist using the considerations presented in Chapter 10—safety, developmental considerations, and so on. Use the checklist to evaluate the appropriateness of the toys shown in the commercials. If you lack information needed to evaluate the toys in relation to any of the items in your checklist, write "Information not available" beside those items. On the basis of this evaluation, would you recommend these toys to care providers in your community?

◆ ◆ ◆ ◆ Look Inward

If you are using this book as a textbook for a course, you will not be asked to share your answers to these questions with your instructor or classmates. These questions are provided to stimulate introspection.

1. Imagine you have been hired as a consultant by a large toy manufacturing company. The company is concerned about making a positive social impact with the toys it manufactures. What advice would you give the company as it plans a new product line for next year? Write a one-page executive summary of your advice.

2. How would you fill in the blanks in these sentences?

    a. I know children need _____, so I will provide _____ in their play environment.

    b. I believe in _____, so the playthings I provide will be _____.

    c. One of my priorities as a care provider is _____, so the play environments I create will include _____.

3. Reflect on your own attitudes toward play in child care settings. Express your attitudes in either (a) a one-page philosophy statement or (b) a list of things you would include in a play environment for the age group of your choice.

References

Albrecht, K.M. (Ed.). (1991). *Quality criteria for school-age child care programs.* Alexandria, VA: Project Home Safe, American Home Economics Association.

Albrecht, K.M., & Plantz, M.C. (Eds.). (1993). *Developmentally appropriate practice in school-age child care programs* (2nd ed.). Dubuque, IA: Kendall/Hunt.

Asher, S.R., & Renshaw, P.D. (1981). Children without friends: Social knowledge and social–skill training. In S.R. Asher & J.M. Gottman (Eds.), *The development of children's friendships* (pp. 273–296). Cambridge, UK: Cambridge University Press.

Barnes, K.E. (1971). Preschool play norms: A replication. *Developmental Psychology, 5,* 99–103.

Bender, J., Elder, B.S., & Flatter, C.H. (1984). Half a childhood: Time for school-age child care. Nashville, TN: School-Age NOTES.

Bloch, M.N. (1992). Critical perspectives on the historical relationship between child development and early childhood education research. In S.A. Kessler & B.B. Swadener (Eds.), *Reconceptualizing the early childhood curriculum: Beginning the dialogue* (pp. 3–20). New York: Teachers College Press.

Bowman, B. (1990). Play in teacher education: The United States perspective. In E. Klugman & S. Smilansky (Eds.), *Children's play and learning: Perspectives and policy implications.* New York: Teachers College Press.

Braiman-Lipson, J., Raub, D.F., & the Editors of Consumer Reports Books. (1988). *Toy buying guide.* Mount Vernon, NY: Consumers Union.

Brainerd, C.J. (1978). *Piaget's theory of intelligence.* Englewood Cliffs, NJ: Prentice-Hall.

Bredekamp, S. (Ed.). (1987). *Developmentally appropriate practice in early childhood programs serving children from birth through age 8.* Washington, DC: National Association for the Education of Young Children.

California Department of Education, Child Development Division. (1993). *Kids' time: A school age care program guide.* Sacramento, CA: Author.

Canadian Child Care Federation. (1994). *National statement on quality child care.* Ottawa, ON: Author.

Choate, J.S. (1993). *Successful mainstreaming.* Boston, MA: Allyn and Bacon.

Colletti-Rizzo, J., & Calkins, B. (1989). Implications for elementary education. In T.A. Rizzo, *Friendship development among children in school* (pp. 129–153). Norwood, NJ: Ablex.

Convention on the rights of the child. In *First call for children* (pp. 43–75). New York: UNICEF.

Corbin, C.B., & Pangrazi, R.P. (1992). Are American children and youth fit? *Research Quarterly for Exercise and Sport, 63,* 96–106.

Damon, W. (1980). Structural-developmental theory and the study of moral development. In M. Windmiller, N. Lambert, & E. Turiel (Eds.), *Moral development and socialization* (pp. 35–68). Boston, MA: Allyn and Bacon.

Dunn, J. (1993). *Young children's close relationships: Beyond attachment.* Newbury Park, CA: Sage.

Durkin, J.F. (1986). *Strategies and contexts in play boundary interactions.* Doctoral dissertation, University of Victoria, Victoria, BC.

Early Childhood Educators of British Columbia. (1994). *Code of ethics.* Vancouver, BC: Author.

Ellis, M.J. (1973). *Why people play.* Englewood Cliffs, NJ: Prentice-Hall.

Erikson, E.H. (1950). *Childhood and society* (2nd ed.). New York: W.W. Norton.

Feeney, S. (1992). Play's place in teacher education. In V.J. Dimidjian (Ed.), *Play's place in public education for young children* (pp. 155–165). Washington, DC: National Education Association.

Feeney, S., Christensen, D., & Moravcik, E. (1991). *Who am I in the lives of children?* (4th ed.). Columbus, OH: Merrill.

Feeney, S., & Kipnis, K. (1989). Code of ethical conduct and statement of commitment. *Young Children, 45* (1), 24–29.

Fewell, R.R., & Kaminski, R. (1988). Play skills development and instruction for young children with handicaps. In S.L. Odom & M.B. Karnes (Eds.), *Early intervention for infants and children with handicaps* (pp. 145–158). Baltimore, MD: Paul H. Brookes.

Freeman, A., & Gray, H. (1989). *Organizing special educational needs: A critical approach.* London: Paul Chapman.

Fromberg, D.P. (1992). A review of research on play. In C. Seefeldt (Ed.), *The early childhood curriculum: A review of current research* (2nd ed.) (pp. 42–84). New York: Teachers College Press.

Frost, J.L. (1985). Introduction. In J.L. Frost & S. Sunderlin (Eds.), *When children play: Proceedings of the international conference on play and play environments* (pp. ix–xi). Wheaton, MD: Association for Childhood Education International.

Frost, J.L. (1992). *Play and playscapes.* Albany, NY: Delmar.

Garvey, C. (1990). *Play.* Cambridge, MA: Harvard University Press.

Gilligan, C. (1982). *In a different voice.* Cambridge, MA: Harvard University Press.

Ginsburg, H., & Opper, S. (1979). *Piaget's theory of intellectual development.* (2nd ed.). Englewood Cliffs, NJ: Prentice-Hall.

Goldschmied, E., & Jackson, S. (1994). *People under three: Young children in day care.* London, UK: Routledge.

Gruber, H.E., & Vonèche, J.J. (Eds.). (1977). *The essential Piaget.* New York: Basic Books.

Guralnick, M.J. (1986). The peer relations of young handicapped and nonhandicapped children. In P.S. Strain, M.J. Guralnick, & H.M. Walker (Eds.), *Children's social behavior: Development, assessment, and modification* (pp. 93–140). Orlando, FL: Academic Press.

Guralnick, M.J. (1990). Major accomplishments and future directions in early childhood mainstreaming. *Topics in Early Childhood Special Education, 10* (2), 1–17.

Haas-Foletta, K., & Cogley, M. (1990). *School-age ideas and activities for after school programs.* Nashville, TN: School-Age NOTES.

Harms, T., & Clifford, R.M. (1980). *Early childhood environment rating scale.* New York: Teachers College Press.

Harms, T., & Clifford, R.M. (1989). *Family day care rating scale.* New York: Teachers College Press.

Harms, T., Cryer, D., & Clifford, R.M. (1990). *Infant/toddler environment rating scale.* New York: Teachers College Press.

Harms, T., Jacobs, E., & White, D. (in press). *School age care environment rating scale.*

Health and Welfare Canada. (1993). *Good books for a good start: Choosing and using children's books in child care.* Ottawa, ON: Author.

Hendrick, J. (1994). *Total learning: Developmental curriculum for the young child* (4th ed.). New York: Merrill.

Honig, A. (1990). The baby—birth to 12 months. In E. Surbeck & M.F. Kelley (Eds.), *Personalizing care with infants, toddlers and families* (pp. 10–22). Wheaton, MD: Association for Childhood Education International.

Honig, A.S., & Lally, J.R. (1981). *Infant caregiving: A design for training.* Syracuse, NY: Syracuse University Press.

Isenberg, J., & Quisenberry, N.L. (1988). *Play: A necessity for all children.* Wheaton, MD: Association for Childhood Education International.

Johnson, T.C. (1993). *Behaviors related to sex and sexuality in preschool children.* (Available from T.C. Johnson, 1101 Fremont Ave., Suite 104, S. Pasadena, CA 91030)

Kelly-Byrne, D. (1989). *A child's play life: An ethnographic study.* New York: Teachers College Press.

King, M.A., Oberlin, A., & Swank, T. (1993). *Creating a child-centered day care environment for two-year-olds.* Springfield, IL: Charles C Thomas.

Kohlberg, L. (1975). The cognitive-developmental approach to moral education. In D. Purpel & K. Ryan (Eds.) *Moral education: It comes with the territory* (pp. 176–195). Berkeley, CA: McCutchan. (Reprinted from *Phi Delta Kappan*, 1975, 670–675)

Krivacska, J.J. (1990). *Designing child sexual abuse prevention programs.* Springfield, IL: Charles C Thomas.

Kuntzleman, C.T., & Reiff, G.G. (1992). The decline in American children's fitness levels. *Research Quarterly for Exercise and Sport, 63,* 107–111.

Kupersmidt, J.B., Coie, J.D., & Dodge, K.A. (1990). The role of poor peer relationships in the development of disorder. In S.R. Asher & J.D. Coie (Eds.), *Peer rejection in childhood* (pp. 274–305). Cambridge, UK: Cambridge University Press.

Landers, C. (1991). Trends in early childhood education and development programs: Perspective from the developing world. In B. Spodek & O.N. Saracho (Eds.), *Issues in early childhood curriculum* (pp. 213–229). New York: Teachers College Press.

Layman, R. (1990). *Current issues: Vol. 1. Child abuse.* Detroit, MI: Omnigraphics.

Leavitt, R.L., & Eheart, B.K. (1985). *Toddler day care: A guide to responsive caregiving.* Lexington, MA: Lexington Books.

Levine, M.C. (Ed.). (1995). *The toy report.* Ottawa, ON: The Canadian Toy Testing Council.

McCallum, M. (1995, March). *The Meadow Lake Tribal Council Indian Child Care Program.* Paper presented at the National Conference on Aboriginal Training Programs in Early Childhood Education, Montreal, QC.

McCollum, J., & McCartan, K. (1988). Research in teacher education: Issues and future directions for early childhood special education. In S.L. Odom & M.B. Karnes (Eds.), *Early intervention for infants and children with handicaps* (pp. 269–286). Baltimore, MD: Paul H. Brookes.

McDonell, L. (1993) *The final report for the school-age training needs analysis project.* Victoria, BC: Province of British Columbia Ministry of Advanced Education, Training and Technology.

Michelson, L., & Mannarino, A. (1986). Social skills training with children: Research and clinical application. In P.S. Strain, M.J. Guralnick, & H.M. Walker (Eds.), *Children's social behavior: Development assessment, and modification* (pp. 373–406). Orlando, FL: Academic Press.

Miller, T.J. (1984). Therapist-child relations in play therapy. In T.D. Yawkey & A.D. Pellegrini (Eds.), *Child's play and play therapy* (pp. 85–103). Lancaster, PA: Technomic.

Monighan-Nourot, M., Scales, B., & Van Hoorn, J., (1987). *Looking at children's play: A bridge between theory and practice.* New York: Teachers College Press.

National Association of Elementary School Principals. (1993). *Standards for quality school-age child care.* Alexandria, VA: Author.

Nucci, L., & Killen, M. (1991). Social interactions in the preschool and the development of moral and social concepts. In B. Scales, M. Almy, A. Nicolopoulou, & S. Ervin-Tripp (Eds.), *Play and the social context of development in early care and education* (pp. 219–233). New York: Teachers College Press.

Parten, M.B. (1932). Social participation among pre-school children. *The Journal of Abnormal and Social Psychology, 27,* 243–269.

Piaget, J. (1972). Some aspects of operations. In M.W. Piers (Ed.), *Play and development* (pp. 15–27). New York: W.W. Norton and Company.

Post, D.L. (1978). Piaget's theory of play: A review of the critical literature. In M.A. Salter (Ed.), *Play: Anthropological perspectives* (pp. 36–41). West Point, NY: Leisure Press.

Powell, D.R. (1994). Parents, pluralism, and the NAEYC statement on developmentally appropriate practice. In B.L. Mallory & R.S. New (Eds.), *Diversity and developmentally appropriate practices* (pp. 166–182). New York: Teachers College Press.

Read, K., Gardner, P., & Mahler, B.C. (1987). *Early childhood programs: Human relationships and learning* (8th ed.). New York: Holt, Rinehart and Winston.

Rizzo, T.A. (1989). *Friendship development among children in school*. Norwood, NJ: Ablex.

Roeher Institute. (1993). *Right off the bat: A study of inclusive child care in Canada*. North York, ON: Author.

Rubin, K.H., Fein, G.G., & Vandenberg, B. (1983). Play. In P.H. Mussen & E.M. Hetherington (Eds.), *Handbook of child psychology* (Vol. 4, pp. 693–774). New York: John Wiley & Sons.

Rubin, K.H., & Howe, N. (1986). Social play and perspective-taking. In G. Fein & M. Rivkin (Eds.), *The young child at play: Reviews of research* (Vol. 4, pp. 113–125). Washington, DC: National Association for the Education of Young Children.

Rubin, K.H., & Pepler, D.J. (1980). The relationship of child's play to social-cognitive growth and development. In H.C. Foot, A.J. Chapman, & J.R. Smith (Eds.), *Friendship and social relations in children* (pp. 209–233). Chichester, UK: John Wiley & Sons.

Saltz, R., & Saltz, E. (1986). Pretend play training and its outcomes. In G. Fein & M. Rivkin (Eds.), *The young child at play: Reviews of research* (Vol. 4, pp. 155–173). Washington, DC: National Association for the Education of Young Children.

Saracho, O.N. (1991). The role of play in the early childhood curriculum. In B. Spodek & O.N. Saracho (Eds.), *Issues in early childhood curriculum* (pp. 86–105). New York: Teachers College Press.

School-Age NOTES. (1994). *After school program catalog*. Nashville, TN: Author.

Selman, R.L. (1981). The child as a friendship philosopher. In S.R. Asher & J.M. Gottman (Eds.), *The development of children's friendships* (pp. 242–272). Cambridge, UK: Cambridge University Press.

Simmons, A. & Porter, M. (1982). *Child's play: Vigorous activities with a limited budget*. Springfield, IL: Charles C Thomas.

Sisson, L.G. (1990). *Kids' club: A school-age program guide for directors*. Nashville, TN: School-Age NOTES.

Smilansky, S. (1968). *The effects of sociodramatic play on disadvantaged preschool children*. New York: John Wiley & Sons.

Smilansky, S. (1990). Sociodramatic play: Its relevance to behavior and achievement in school. In E. Klugman & S. Smilansky (Eds.), *Children's play and learning: Perspectives and policy implications* (pp. 18–42). New York: Teachers College Press.

Smith, P.K., & Syddall, S. (1978). Play and non-play tutoring in pre-school children: Is it play or tutoring which matters? *British Journal of Educational Psychology, 48,* 315–325.

Spodek, B. (1991). Early childhood curriculum and cultural definitions of knowledge. In B. Spodek & O.N. Saracho (Eds.), *Issues in early childhood curriculum* (pp. 1–20). New York: Teachers College Press.

Sutton-Smith, B. (1994, October). UNESCO-OMEP project. In V. Fronczek (Chair), *In celebration of childhood: The importance of play in child development.* Paper presented at the meeting of the Society for Children and Youth of BC, Vancouver, BC.

Travers, J.F., Elliott, S.N., & Kratochwill, T.R. (1993). *Educational psychology.* Madison, WI: W.C.B. Brown & Benchmark.

van Raalte, D.L. (1995). The MicMac/Maliseet Child Care Curriculum. Paper presented at the National Conference on Aboriginal Training Programs in Early Childhood Education, March, Montreal, QC.

Vandenberg, B.R. (1986). Beyond the ethology of play. In A.W. Gottfried & C.C. Brown (Eds.), *Play interactions* (pp. 3–11). Lexington, MA: Lexington Books.

Wehman, P. (1978). Play skill development. In N. H. Fallen & J. E. McGovern (Eds.), *Young children with special needs* (pp. 277–303). Columbus, OH: Charles E. Merrill.

Windmiller, M., Lambert, N., & Turiel, E. (Eds.). (1980). *Moral development and socialization.* Boston, MA: Allyn and Bacon.

Wortham, S.C. (1985). A history of outdoor play 1900–1985: Theories of play and play environments. In J.L. Frost & S. Sunderlin (Eds.), *When children play: Proceedings of the international conference on play and play environments* (pp. 3–7). Wheaton, MD: Association for Childhood Education International.

Index

A

Abuse
  indicators, 153-155
  response of care providers, 154-155
ACEI, *See* Association for Childhood
  Education International
Active listening, 92
Active observing, 4-6
Administration, 41-44
Advisory group, 59-60
Advocacy
  for inclusiveness, 38-39, 141-143
  on behalf of children, 141
Association for Childhood Education
International, 142
Attitudes
  of care providers, 12, 36
  toward play, 7

B

Behavior
  guiding children's, 126-127
Beliefs
  of care provider, 12, 82-83

C

Care providers
  as curriculum developers, 58
  definition, 2, 83-84
  for infants and toddlers, 82-83
  relationships with parents, 36, 39-41
  response to hurtful play, 150
  response to children's sexual curiosity, 152
  response to indicators of abuse, 154-155
  responsibilities to parents, 39-41
  role in the play environments, 26, 74-85,
  101-103, 124, 160-165
Child care profession, 8, 10-11
Child development
  alternative perspectives, 73
  theories, 17-28, 68-73, 90-100, 114-124
Cognitive development,
  of infants and toddlers, 71-73
  of preschoolers, 97-98
  of school-age children, 23, 119-121
Community
  child care views, 59
  elements of, 53-60
  quality of life, 51
  values, 58-61

Conservation, 120
Convention on the Rights of the Child, 143
Crises, 69-70
Curriculum, 58

D

Decision making
  by care providers, 3, 104-105
  by children, 102, 124
Developmentally appropriate practice,
  NAEYC definition, 6-11, 32, 68
Development psychology
  and child care, 8-10
  and play, 9-11
Domains
  of development, 68
    cognitive, 71-73, 97-98, 119-121
    emotional, 69-70, 90-92, 116-117
    moral, 98-100, 121-124
    physical, 68-69, 115-116
    social, 70-71, 93-97, 117-119
    spiritual, 68
Dramatic play, 50, 80, 133
Durkin, J., 93-95

E

Early Childhood Educators of British
Columbia
  code of ethics, 105
Emotional development
  of infants and toddlers, 69-70
  of preschoolers, 90-92
  of school-age children, 116
Empathic play, 97
Erikson, E.
  crises, 69-70, 90-91, 116
  theory, 69-70, 90, 116-117
Ethical considerations
  in selection of playthings, 104-105, 162-
  164. *See also* Playthings, selections
Ethical decision making, 3, 104
Ethical dilemma, 42
Ethical domain, 3, 26, 103, 162-163
Ethical practice, 2, 26, 103-106
Ethical principles
  personal, 3, 103
  professional, 3, 105
Ethics, codes, 105-106

tutoring, 135-136
value of, 165, 167
Play environments
ACEI position, 142
and peer interactions, 93, 117-119
for babies, 75-77
for infants and toddlers, 74-75
for one-year-olds, 78-79
for preschoolers, 101-103
for school-age children, 124
for two-year-olds, 79-80
physical elements, 74-75
social elements, 74-75
use of local materials, 102
Playgrounds, 114
Playthings
and creativity, 164
appropriate, 165-166
play value, 165
selection, 159-167. *See also* Ethical considerations
Preschoolers
cognitive development, 97-98
emotional development, 90-92
moral development, 98-100
physical development, 90
social development, 93-95
Program planning, 4
Project Home Safe, 9

Q

Qualities of care providers, 39, 83-84
Quality of child care
assessment instruments, 12, 25, 50, 101
CCCF position, 11, 50, 81
local appropriateness, 4, 51
NAEYC position, 6
Project Home Safe position, 9, 11

R

Reading to children, 98
Relationships
among care providers, 51, 75
care provider—child, 2, 36, 51
care provider—parent, 36, 39-41
effect of, 51
quality of, 51
Research literature, 4-10, 136
Research models, 35, 70, 99
Research practitioner
active observing, 4-6, 139
attitude, 6
sharing knowledge, 5
questions for, 5

S

Safety, 80-82
School-age children
and play, 110-129
care providers for, 126
choosing inactivity, 112
cognitive development, 23, 119-121
diversity among, 125
emotional development, 116
moral development, 121-124
physical development, 115
concerns about, 115-116
social development, 117-119
Self-esteem, 117
Selman, R.L.
stages of friendship, 137-138
Smilansky, S.
research assumptions, 134
research findings, 132-133
Social conventions, 99-101
Social development
of infants and toddlers, 70-71
of preschoolers, 92-95
of school-age children, 117-119
Social impact of playthings, 164
Social participation, 93-97, 139
Social skills, 140-141
Sociodramatic play, 80, 132-133

T

Theories
building, 18, 27
of play, 18-26
cognitive-developmental, 23, 71-73
instinct, 19
limitations of, 26-27
psychoanalytic, 20-21
recapitulation, 19
recreation, 19
surplus energy, 19
third-generation, 27-28
purpose, 18
testing, 18, 24
Treasure baskets, 77

V

Values, 58-61